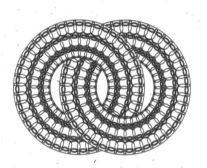

ITALIAN
BLOOD

ITALIAN BLOOD

A MEMOIR

DENISE
CIMBARO TOLAN

CAVANKERRY
PRESS

CavanKerry Press Ltd.
Fort Lee, New Jersey
www.cavankerrypress.org

Publisher's Cataloging-in-Publication Data
provided by Five Rainbows Cataloging Services
Names: Tolan, Denise, author. | Romo, Ito, writer of foreword.
Title: Italian blood / Denise Tolan ; foreword by Ito Romo.
Description: Fort Lee, NJ : CavanKerry Press, 2023.
Identifiers: ISBN 978-1-933880-95-2 (paperback) | ISBN 978-1-960327-25-3 (ebook)
Subjects: LCSH: Women—Biography. | Italian Americans—Biography. | Family
    violence. | Families. | Autobiography. | Essays. | BISAC: BIOGRAPHY &
    AUTOBIOGRAPHY / Women. | BIOGRAPHY & AUTOBIOGRAPHY / Survival. |
    BIOGRAPHY & AUTOBIOGRAPHY / Cultural, Ethnic & Regional / General.
Classification: LCC E184.I8 T65 2023 (print) | LCC E184.I8 (ebook) | DDC
    973/.0451—dc23.

Cover photo: "Mount Vesuvius, active" from Library of Congress,
    LC-DIG-ppmsca-015616.
Interior text design by Ryan Scheife, Mayfly Design
First Edition 2023, Printed in the United States of America

 Made possible by funds from the New Jersey State Council on the Arts, a partner agency of the National Endowment for the Arts.

CavanKerry Press is grateful for the support it receives from the New Jersey State Council on the Arts, the National Endowment for the Arts, and the New Jersey Arts and Culture Renewal Fund.

In addition, CavanKerry Press gratefully acknowledges generous grants and emergency support received during the COVID-19 pandemic from the following funders:

The Academy of American Poets

Community of Literary Magazines and Presses

National Book Foundation

New Jersey Council for the Humanities

New Jersey Economic Development Authority

Northern New Jersey Community Foundation

The Poetry Foundation

US Small Business Administration

For Bill, who is my beginning, middle, and end.

This story contains content that might be troubling to some readers, including, but not limited to, violence, partner abuse, child abuse, gun violence, death threats, and PTSD. Please be mindful of these and other possible triggers and seek assistance if needed from the resources on page 111.

CONTENTS

FOREWORD

As I turned page after page of Denise Tolan's memoir, *Italian Blood*, I could not help but think of a telenovela I watched as a kid growing up on the border called *Muchacha Italiana Viene a Casarse*. It's the story of a young Italian woman who is convinced, via letters and photos, into traveling from her small Italian village to Mexico to marry. Her problems begin when she and her younger sister arrive in Mexico City, and she realizes that the man in the photos she's crossed the ocean to marry is actually an old man many times her age named Don Vittorio (yes, this was old-school catfishing). Now, in a foreign country, she is left with two terrible choices: marry old Don Vittorio or take the only job she can find as a maid of a wealthy Mexican family and fall in love with the family's only bachelor son, who, by the way, also falls in love with her. You can imagine the drama that ensues. In the end, as always, after much theatrical trial and tribulation, they marry and live happily ever after.

So, two things happen to me when I read the stories of Tolan's life: (1) I have to keep reminding myself that it's not fiction, that it's not a nostalgically entertaining soap opera from my youth, and (2) I can't help but think about the affinity of image that Tolan and I share—perhaps by having lived right in the middle of two worlds: "American"/Italian, "American"/Mexican. Maybe it's the bilingual upbringing and what that does to our sensibilities. Whatever the reason may be, Denise Tolan's *Italian Blood* both alarmed and comforted me, and in doing so, startled me with its beauty. This new American memoir is both an experience lived as well as an experience seen from afar, from another "America," Tolan's painful life, bled honestly onto the page.

She writes,

> At a stoplight a family in the car next to us looked into our
> truck window. I was proud of what they saw—my beautiful

mother wearing fresh lipstick, the American Eskimo dog licking my chin, and my father singing loudly and beautifully with the windows wide open—"*When the moon hits your eye like a big pizza pie, that's amore.*" I would have been jealous if I'd been in the other car.

This Italian American gothic of a happy family is far from the desperate reality of Tolan's family life. But it's the juxtaposition of this ideal American family to the painfully dark and brutal reality of her experience that moves the darkness from the shocking to the sublime.

I could do my best to retell a scene during which Tolan tells us, "Over the years, I'd heard my father threaten to kill my mother if she ever left him. Sometimes he even said he'd kill us kids first, then leave her alive so she would have to live knowing we were dead because of her." Or I could show you how when Tolan was an adult, gone from home and married already, she'd talk with her mother several times a day, the first of these calls from her mother early in the morning. She writes, "It was her way of telling me she'd made it through the night without my father waking in the dark to exorcise his demons using her body as a sacrament." Or how she tells us, "My brother and I slept on our stomachs so we wouldn't see it coming. Our dad. His gun." But there's more. Tolan's family fear is old. A fear inherited, we find out.

In a post on social media, Tolan recently posted a photo of three generations of the women in her family sitting around her grandmother's table in Udine, a tiny town in Italy, and along with the photo, she commented, "there is happiness on our faces. Around that table, we are safe. Around her table, hearts beat together with Italian blood." *Italian Blood* is also the story of the long line of Italian women that came before Tolan, women caught in a multigenerational cycle of spousal abuse in its most frightening and violent form. And, again, the honest precision of scene, whether in a home of a San Antonio suburb or around the marble table of the ancient kitchen of an ancestral home, the intensity of the brutality is real and surprising.

Yet, Tolan, makes us laugh—granted, a nervous laugh, but a laugh nonetheless. Almost as if gallows humor had inadvertently made its way into Tolan's young life without her even knowing it, and provided her, perhaps as she writes about it retrospectively, with the disengagement, the separation from reality needed to survive. Take the part where she writes that as a teenager, she literally planned to kill her father,

> I figured if I babysat every weekend for a month, I could buy the go-go boots. My breasts were already larger than most girls my age. Maybe, with makeup, I could get a job at the Squirrel Cage. . . . I spent weekends at the public library researching social security benefits my mother and brother could get from my dead father. I wasn't sure I would get them too, since I was the one who killed him, but I had the phantom job at the Squirrel Cage anyway.

Now I nervously laugh.

I will not tell you how this very real telenovela ends. I will not tell you that she lives happily ever after. But I will tell you this, Denise Tolan's *Italian Blood* is a bracingly beautiful, unconditionally honest depiction of the Italian American experience in the United States written in a voice that does not flinch. Listen to her. She knows things you don't.

Ito Romo,
author of *The Border Is Burning*
and *El Puente / The Bridge*
March 2023

Prima Parte: Il Sangue Non e Acqua

PART ONE: BLOOD IS NOT WATER

NEVER TWO WITHOUT THE THREE

When my mother moved from Italy to the United States, she remembered to pack her superstitions with her. "Be careful," she would tell the young mothers in New Jersey grocery stores near our apartment. "When you think about a food, don't touch your baby's face or it will leave a mark." My mother would pat the women's shoulders and smile like she had given them a treasured gift they could take home and put in their china cabinets.

Her sayings were gifted to her family as well. If I bumped my elbow on the barstool in front of our kitchen, she'd raise an eyebrow. If I hit my elbow on the same barstool again, she would stop whatever she was doing to look me in the eye.

"*Attenzione!*" she'd say. "Never two without the three."

I'd walk around the house for a while, hyperaware of the stupid stool, because more than anything else I wanted to prove her wrong. But if I took the corner too fast and hit my elbow on the stool again, I'd hear her voice from across the sink. "See? The three. *'E la verita.*" It's the truth.

The truth is I bought into her superstitions completely. I still dread things happening in twos. When my son was six, a teenager slammed into our car as we were turning onto our street. The next week, a block away from our house, a young driver ran a stop sign and hit my husband's car. There was the two. I was almost giddy when my mother told me her neighbor had been hit in the parking lot of the grocery store by a kid who lived on their street. The third!

————

The year I got married I also got pregnant. It turned out to be a heartbreaking ectopic pregnancy that began with a joyful visit to the doctor's office to hear the baby's heartbeat and ended with an emergency surgery to remove the fetus growing inside my fallopian tube.

I was depressed after the surgery. I hadn't been sure I was ready to be pregnant, but I was sure I wasn't ready to lose a baby either. A few weeks later, as my mother was getting ready to fly to Italy to visit her mother, I decided to fly from Dallas to San Antonio to say good-bye to her and get away from my thoughts.

"I don't like you flying so soon after surgery," my mother said.

I ignored her and ignored the cramping in my stomach as well. I wanted to feel her arms around me, hear her say I would have another baby one day, that I was not a failure for losing one. Her voice was more powerful than any pain I was feeling.

Besides that, since my nona didn't have a phone in Italy, I would not be able to talk to my mother for weeks. We usually spoke on the phone three times a day. In the morning, she would call me to make sure I was awake and ready for work. It was her way of telling me she'd made it through the night without my father waking in the dark to exorcise his demons using her body as a sacrament.

Before I left work in the afternoon, I called my mom. We'd chat about what we'd eaten that day or who we might have seen or the weather. It was a verbal end-of-the-day glass of wine. In the evening, before we went to sleep, her voice on the phone was almost a call to prayer. I imagined her safe in her bed. I'd whisper a Hail Mary so my father would stay in another room.

Our phone calls were an incantation that would be broken while she was gone. I needed a weekend to bank her voice until she returned.

The second I saw my mother at the airport, I could see things were not going well. She looked tired and her hair was flat in the back like she had slept on her pillow all night without moving once. She was usually very self-conscious about our genetically flat heads.

"*Lo so*," my mother said, hugging me and trying to fluff up her hair at the same time. "I know. It's been a bad day."

We held hands while we walked to get my luggage. Waiting at the airport carousel, my mother looked around and nudged me in the ribs. "All these people and no one is dressed nice. Maybe all their good clothes are in the suitcases."

We giggled like friends in a school lunchroom. It felt good to laugh with her again, to hold her hand, to spend a few light moments alone before she would finally have to let me in on why it had been a bad day. All I could assume was that a bad day usually meant my father was in one of his moods.

On the way to the parking garage, my mother was unusually quiet. I let it go and followed her to the car.

When I spotted the pistachio-colored Pinto wagon in the lot, I had to laugh.

"Mom, are those decorative pillows in the backseat?"

"Why not," she said. "It's so boring back there."

I placed my suitcase in the trunk and asked if she wanted me to drive. She shook her head no.

After paying for parking, we headed for the highway. I was surprised when she turned right instead of left, toward our house.

"Mom?"

"Your brother is in the hospital," she said. "We need to see what the X-rays say."

I was afraid to ask much more. I leaned back in the seat and looked out the window at the familiar interstate I'd driven so many times before. My brother was in the hospital. Over the years, my father had caused physical damage to most of our family, but a hospital visit was not common. Then again, I understood that sometimes my father could be the catalyst for catastrophe without laying a hand on anyone.

I turned to look at my mother, but she was focused on the road, lost in her own worry. I let her drive and wondered what we would find when we got to the hospital.

––––––

My mother exited the highway and turned onto the two-lane road that led to the hospital. She let out a sigh. I thought the sigh was because she was happy to be off the highway, but she looked at me and sighed again.

"Your brother bought a motorcycle yesterday because your father took the car away from him. I hate motorcycles, but your brother needed a way to get to work. He said it was all he could afford. What could I do?"

"Why did Dad take his car?"

"Who knows?" my mother said. "He was mad because your brother was someplace and somebody splashed two of his tires."

My mother spoke English with a heavy accent, but sometimes words outran her brain. "You mean slashed? Like cut them?"

"Yes," she said. "Your father said your brother was not taking care of things and so he sold the car."

"But wasn't Greg paying him every month?"

My mother waved her hand in the air and sighed. That meant there was no use trying to explain why my father did the things he did.

It was difficult to explain my father. He was a language we weren't quite fluent in. When we were little, we always had the newest toys. My father had grown up poor, he said, though he never said much more. He bought us a new toy each Friday, his eyes as happy with the acquisition as ours. He was the dad who did things like play board games and take us to little country flea markets and read comic books with us. Some kids on our street even said they wished he was their father.

But this was the same father who'd wake us in the middle of the night to chase violence. If a tornado warning came on the news, he'd yell for us to get in the car, then follow the clouds. Or he'd drive us hours away from home to survey the aftermath of a hurricane. Sometimes he'd have my mother sign us out of school while he waited in the car ready to take us to the scene of a mudslide where houses slipped down hills like toy cars sliding off a table.

Some nights, he was the natural disaster, hurling heavy objects across the room like they were toys and circling us with the bluster of a wind god. We woke in the mornings to find overturned tables, objects that once graced the surfaces covering our floor like a construction site.

"So the accident?" I prodded.

My mother pulled into the hospital parking lot, removed her sunglasses, and leaned forward, her shoulders squared with the steering wheel. She was determined not to lose out on finding the best place to park. I noticed tense lines forming a trench from her shoulders to her neck.

"Are you okay, Mom?"

"When your brother came home with that machine, I was so mad at him. Why would he scare me this way?"

"You just said—he needed something to get around with, Mom. He's nineteen. A motorcycle is all he could afford."

"Yes," she said. "But every time he drives now, I have to worry. And he does this right before I go to Italy. I got mad at him."

"You should have gotten mad at Dad when he took away the car."

She was silent. I wasn't sure if she thought I was right or wrong.

"Anyway," she went on, "I was yelling at your brother when your father came home. He saw the motorcycle and saw I was upset and then he got mad at Greg. Your father tried to throw the motorcycle on the ground, and your brother tried to get away. Greg doesn't know anything about motorcycles and when he left so fast he ran into the mailbox. His knee hit the bricks and he fell and hit his head too. *Mio Dio*, there was so much blood. Charles from next door took Greg to the hospital so I could come get you."

"Why didn't Dad take him to the hospital?"

"Who knows?" my mother said, shrugging her shoulders as if I'd asked her what was on sale at the grocery store that week. "There was so much confusion."

By the time we got to the hospital, my father was there. He gave me a hug and told us that Greg was getting stitches in his forehead. The doctor said his knee was swollen and badly cut, but he would heal just fine.

"That kid better take some motorcycle lessons," my dad said. I noticed a long, ragged streak of dried blood on the sleeve of his stiff white Arrow shirt.

"Where's Charles?" I asked.

"Who?" he said.

My mother pinched me so I would shut up.

When they called my dad back to wheel my brother out, I turned to my mom. "Why do we let him get away with this crap?"

"He's being nice now," my mother said. "*Lascia stare.*" Let it go.

We always let it go. It was almost a family mantra.

"You look so pale," she said. "I'll make you some good sauce for the gnocchi tonight, yes?"

And just like that, I let it go too. My mother was leaving for Italy. My brother was in the hospital. My stomach was cramping. There was too much for me to hold.

————

Back at the house, my mother began to boil potatoes for the gnocchi. It was always my special welcome home meal. I watched her cook while I sat on the barstool I had bumped into so many times as a kid. My brother was on the couch, ice on his knee and heavy meds in his stomach. My dad paced the concrete patio in the backyard like a dog in a cage—never a good sign.

I went back to my mom's bedroom and dozed on her bed, trying to focus on anything besides the cramping in my stomach. Soon I heard raised voices and the sound of a pot hitting the wall, and I knew there would be no good sauce for dinner.

My brother walked into the room, shut the door, and sat at the edge of the bed.

"Beppino," I heard my mother say before Greg shut the door. It was her pet name for my father. It was always a last-ditch effort to stop the inevitable.

"He's mad because she let Charles take me to the hospital," Greg said.

My face burned with shame. "Shit. I shouldn't have said anything about Charles at the hospital."

My brother sighed. "He's been this way all day. If it wasn't that, it would have been something else."

I nodded. I was twenty-three and my brother was nineteen. We still blamed ourselves for our father's behavior—still tried to figure out what we did right and where we went wrong—still didn't dare say out loud that there was something wrong with him.

We listened to the shouting and the sound of objects being thrown and tried not to look at each other. I heard a slap and knew it would never come from my mother. I stayed on the bed. My brother stayed on the edge of the bed. I knew we were both thinking *just let this be over soon.*

At some point, we fell asleep. My mother woke us up with cups of tomato soup and grilled cheese sandwiches.

"You two eat," she said. "Everything is fine. Your father is taking a nap on the couch and I am going to take a quick shower. We will start the day over, huh?"

I looked at the clock by the side of the bed. Seven pm. My brother and I nodded, like puppets being manipulated from somewhere else.

My brother ate, then left to take his medicine. I drifted back to sleep until I heard my mother calling my name. When I got up, I felt a rush of warm liquid run down my legs. I ran to the toilet in my mother's bathroom afraid to look between my legs to see what happened. When I looked up, I saw my mother in the shower with the water turned off, blood spurting from her leg like a sprinkler in the front yard.

"My varicose vein," she said. "I hit it on the spout."

We started laughing then—her naked in the shower and me on the toilet. Then I started crying and she went into action.

"It's going to be okay. You get a towel, a dark one, and put it in your underwear. There are pads in your old bathroom. Give me a towel for my leg. When you have the pads on, go get your father to take me to the hospital. And don't forget to put your towel in the sink with cold water when you are through."

"Really, Mom?"

"No use to ruin a good towel."

I took a towel and threw it between my legs, then grabbed a towel for my mother's leg. The bathroom looked like a scene from a gruesome Halloween movie.

"Oh my God," my mother said, looking at the toilet after I got up.

"It's just a heavy period from after the surgery," I told my mother. "I'm fine."

I wasn't sure I was fine. After the miscarriage and the surgery, the doctor assured me I would bleed lightly for just a few days and then I could return to normal activities. But this was anything but normal bleeding.

As I watched my mother's leg pumping blood onto the towel I'd just handed her, I decided to tell her the small lie to keep her from worrying about me.

While my father took my mother to the hospital, I went back to bed. I thought about a road trip we had taken to Canada to visit relatives on my mother's side. My mother, who always had awful, heavy periods, was having an extra heavy flow on the trip. She'd asked my father to stop at rest areas more frequently than usual so she could check her pads, but he grew more and more annoyed at the slowdowns as the day went on. When we finally stopped at a rest area for dinner, my mother held me back.

"Go to the bathroom and get some paper towels. Put cold water on them and a little soap. When your father is not looking, pretend you have to go to the car for your book and then wipe the seat for me."

I was nine and nervous. When I opened the passenger side door instead of the back door to get my book, my dad's suspicions were aroused. I saw three spots of blood on the car seat, forming an almost perfect triangle. Two of the spots were the size of quarters, but one was the size of an Oreo cookie. Before I could even touch the seat, my father was there.

In the end, some people in the rest area called the police. The cops took my father for a walk to cool him off and my mother scrubbed the seat while they were gone. No matter how many times over the years my mother tried to clean the seat, faint circles of blood remained like a design in the fabric. My father reminded us whenever we got in the car how much money he would lose when he sold it because my mother was a filthy pig.

I had at least six pads in my underwear and two towels folded underneath me, but I got up every ten minutes to make sure I didn't get any blood on my mother's sheets.

When my parents came home from the hospital, my father stopped short when he saw me.

Soon I heard him in the bathroom, opening cabinets and rooting around on the shelves. My mother walked in the bedroom and sat by my side.

"Where's your father?"

I pointed to the bathroom.

He came back shaking a thermometer, then handed it to me.

"You have a temperature of a hundred and three," my father said. "Back to the hospital."

"I told him about the blood," my mother said. "I was worried."

"Never two without the three," I said.

She cocked her head, like a dog hearing a familiar sound. "*Cosa sai fare?* What can you do? What's true is true."

I put five towels on the seat of the car before my father drove me to the hospital. The doctors in San Antonio told me I had toxemia from placenta left behind after my surgery in Dallas. They gave me the choice to have another surgery that night in San Antonio, or to fly back to Dallas first thing in the morning and have it there. I opted to fly back to Dallas to be with my husband. It was where I felt safe. He was where I was safe.

By the time we got to my parents' house, it was after three am. My flight to Dallas was scheduled for six am. The hospital had given me drugs to slow the bleeding and stop the pain, but I couldn't sleep.

My father came to check on me often. Beneath his dark eyebrows were soft, concerned eyes.

"Hey little girl," he said, kneeling by the bed. It reminded me of when I was six and had the mumps and my father sat on the floor reading me *National Velvet*. He shared very few childhood memories with me, but he told me then how he never had money for lunch in school, so he would go to the library and read books by Louis L'Amour and Zane Grey.

When my parents bought their first house, there were bookcases along the fireplace in the living room. He worked an extra job delivering papers early in the morning so he could buy a collection of Zane Grey books for those shelves. The spines were gray, the lettering burgundy.

One night, when I was about fourteen, I came to the living room and picked up a Zane Grey novel. My mother walked past me into the kitchen. My father, sitting in the recliner watching baseball, jumped up like he'd been stung by a bee, ran to the kitchen, and grabbed her by the hair. When I got to the kitchen, her head was in the sink.

"Who did this?" he yelled, over and over. "Look. Look. Right there."

I followed his finger as he circled a small chip on the bottom of the enamel sink. He began banging my mother's head on the chipped area until drops of blood splattered the sink like dozens of new tiny chips.

I screamed until he let go of her hair and then I threw the book at the back of his head. He caught the book and looked at it, then me, as if I'd harmed an animal.

Now those same eyes looked at me with concern.

"How you doing, little girl?" he asked again, from under the same eyebrows. Through the same eyes.

———

It seemed like I had just closed my eyes when my father woke me to leave for the airport. As I was sitting up, I saw blood in the shape of a crescent moon stretching from his pinky finger to his wrist bone.

How ironic, I thought, that out of all of us today, he was the only one with blood on his hands.

DIVISIBLE BY THIRTEEN

Italy, 1973

I turned thirteen twice that year.

The first celebration began at five o'clock in the morning after my brother, our mother, and I carried our suitcases downstairs and stacked them by my nona's front door. The suitcases were lined up like we soon would be in the plane—my brother by the window, me in the middle, and my mother at the aisle. We were flying back to Texas after five weeks in Italy.

"*Siediti*," my nona said, pointing to the heavy chair at the head of her kitchen table. She placed a small Italian cream cake in front of me. "*Buon compleanno.*"

A used, nearly transparent candle glowed in the center of the cake like a torch in the Arctic. After I blew out the weak flame, we took turns passing around a fork, each of us taking a small bite of the sweet, white dessert.

My mother took a bite, then made a face to let us know she thought the cake was too sweet. She walked to the stove for a cup of black coffee.

Like a magician pulling a rabbit from a hat, my nona reached into her apron pocket and held out a package wrapped in gold foil. She moved the cake and put the box in its place. "*Per te*," she said. For you.

I tried not to tear the shiny gold paper as I opened the present. I wanted to take it home to use as a bookmark—a souvenir. Inside the wrapped package was a pink plastic box with scalloped edges that opened like I imagined a clamshell might. On a creamy satin pillow inside the box was a tiny gold cross. My mother turned from the stove and watched as I held up the cross for her and my brother to see.

"*Quanti carati?*" my mother asked.

"*Diciotto carati. Cos 'altro?*"

"Your nona bought you good eighteen karat gold," my mother said, scolding me as if I'd already done something wrong with the gift. "You better take care of it, *capito?*" You hear me?

I nodded reverently. I didn't know the difference between eighteen karat gold and any other gold, but clearly there was a big one. The tiny cross suddenly felt heavy in my hand. My nona took a used tissue from her apron pocket and wiped her nose. Then she pulled a thin gold chain from the other pocket. I threaded the cross on the chain and handed it back to her to clasp behind my neck.

While she tried to connect the chain from one end to the other, I held the hair off my neck and felt the familiar sting of building tears. I cried because the cross was the first piece of nice jewelry I'd ever received, and I knew she must have saved for a long time to buy this gift for me. I cried because I realized when she reached into her apron how her rounded spine made it seem as if she were forever looking into her pockets. I cried because when I saw her again next year, she'd be even older. Another year seemed like a lot for her to endure.

"No cry," she said, turning me so she could see how the cross looked on my neck. "No cry," she said in English with her heavy Italian accent, rubbing the back of my head, pushing my face into her shoulder. "No cry," she said again and again. I was grateful she never said the words in Italian. Somehow the word *cry* was easier to hear in English. It didn't belong in Italian where we never had to say things like that.

In the background my mother held a camera in front of her eye as if she intended to take a picture, but changed her mind at the last minute. The only pictures my mother wanted were of happy moments when everyone was well dressed and smiling. During my mother's weekly canasta game, her friends threw down pictures along with their cards. Who had the prettiest daughter, the richest son-in-law, the high card? My mother caught me and my nona in a moment of melancholy. This was not a photo she would win with.

The taxi idled by my nona's front door while my mother finished the call to my father. She was making sure he knew what time our plane would arrive in San Antonio. Before hanging up she held the phone out for me.

"I'm not wishing you a happy birthday yet," my father said. "It's still August 17th here. We'll celebrate when you land in Texas. Then you'll be a real thirteen-year-old."

I fingered the soft gold of my new cross as we headed in the taxi toward the bus station, then took the bus to the airport. I boarded the plane in Milan as a thirteen-year-old, but somewhere in the air between Italy and Texas time fell apart in a way I didn't understand and for a while, I was twelve again.

Texas

When we landed in San Antonio, Texas, my father hugged me before anyone else. "Now I'll say happy birthday," he said, handing me a perfectly square, wrapped box. The box turned out to contain a round Panasonic ball and chain radio. Nothing my father handed out was ever what it seemed. I could almost picture the radio being used as an object for him to throw one night when he was angry. But today, he smiled as I held the gift.

"A grown-up gift for a grown-up girl," he said.

So much irony in that box.

He wore a pair of slacks with a collared shirt tucked in and his good shoes without laces. He looked like most of the Italian men we had just left behind: dark wavy hair, confident eyes, a cruel jaw. My brother and I walked together toward the parking lot while my father and mother walked behind. They held hands and smiled shyly at one another like a couple of teenagers who'd been separated for the summer while they attended camp.

When my brother and I spotted our dog Bianco sitting like a chauffeur in the driver's seat of my dad's truck, we began to run. I opened the door and Bianco licked me crazily, hungrily, without restraint. He had been my twelfth birthday present. My brother got in the truck and held up an empty McDonald's bag. Bianco sniffed it.

"You ate at McDonalds?" my brother asked, suspiciously. My father hated McDonalds.

"The dog likes their milk shakes," he said, shrugging. "What are you going to do?"

We all laughed. The moment felt like a scene from a situation comedy I hoped to watch again and again. In the tight backseat of the truck I held Bianco and tried to smell the milk shake already dry in the fur around his snout.

At a stoplight a family in the car next to us looked into our truck window. I was proud of what they saw—my beautiful mother wearing fresh lipstick, the American Eskimo dog licking my chin, and my father singing loudly and beautifully with the windows wide open—"*When the moon hits your eye like a big pizza pie, that's amore.*" I would have been jealous if I'd been in the other car.

For the first few days of my thirteenth year, I thought our yearly rituals might have worked—the candles, the prayers, the trip to Saint Anthony's grotto. Then my father woke in the middle of the night. He might have tripped over the dog or an old memory, but whatever hit him started the familiar descent into his unique brand of madness.

Italy

During the school year my mom worked in a daycare center so she could buy the plane tickets that would take us back to Italy every year. My father never went. He had to work, or watch the dog, or be home in case of an emergency. No one ever pushed too hard. Italy was ours.

We always left Texas in July, flying from San Antonio to Atlanta, then to Milan. In Milan we boarded a small airplane to Ronchi. From Ronchi, we took a bus to Udine. The first few days at my nona's house were recovery days from the travel. We happily confined ourselves to my nona's dark, quiet row house playing *briscola*, eating handmade gnocchi, and watching television shows we hadn't seen in a year. In the mornings, my mother would carry a warm pitcher of water upstairs so we could take a sponge bath. There was a toilet downstairs, but no shower. We adapted quickly.

Left on my own, I would sneak into my nona's bedroom, open her armoire, and look at her slips. She had folded them all so beautifully.

Between each slip was a delicate piece of tissue paper like the kind fine department stores wrap clothes in.

A few years earlier, while I'd waited for my nona to dress, she'd asked me to hand her a slip.

"Nona," I'd said, startled to see so many slips in her drawer. "*Ce ne sono troppi.*" There are too many.

"Look on the left and count three slips down. That's the one I need. *Avanti su*—come on."

When I told my mother about the slips, she shook her head as if the story was one she hadn't heard in a long time. "She always said it was important to be able to find her slips even in the dark. I guess it was from the war when they had no electricity. She puts the paper in between each slip to help her count," my mother said, then sighed. "Slips are the only nice things your nona ever owned."

When I was sure no one was looking for me, I'd unfold my nona's delicate slips and wrap them around my shoulders like they were mink stoles. They felt rich and a little decadent. I pretended I was the heroine in an old foreign film who had done something brave to keep her family together. In my movie, we never went back to Texas.

Across the street from my nona's house was the University of Udine. I'd sit for hours in her bedroom window with a slip on my shoulder watching the students come and go. I studied them, trying to figure out what made them Italian and me so American. Was it the way they kept talking as they greeted each other with a kiss on one cheek then the other? Was it the way they held their chins slightly upward as if to say they were listening, but still believed their own ideas were the best? Was it the ease in their step as they walked the ancient brick streets never looking for places they might trip?

In Italy, people would always stop my brother and me and ask, "*Americani?*" Even when we answered in perfect Italian they would smile, "*Si, si. Americani.*" In the afternoons I walked up and down Via Superiore pretending I had a mink stole on my shoulders, mimicking the chin and the walk. I wanted to be a part of this motherland so when I returned to the fatherland *it* would feel like the foreign place.

After a week or more in Italy, when my mother must have sensed a shift in our energy, she'd wake us early in the morning to begin our annual pilgrimage to the grotto of Saint Anthony. Even though by then my brother and I were usually ready to leave the house, we were never excited about the first stop of the trip, which was in the small village of Ciseriis.

"I hate this place. It's so boring," my brother would say, looking out the window of the bus. A wooden picnic table beneath a chestnut tree was the marker letting us know we were getting close to the village.

"*Sta zitto*," my mother would whisper, pointing to my brother with her long, skinny finger. "Ciseriis is our village. This is where our people come from. This is where my mother was born, where your sister was born. *Ricordatente."* You remember.

This stop was important to my mother and my nona, but don't look for Ciseriis in a guidebook. The bus drops passengers off in front of Chiesa di Ciseriis because there is nowhere else to drop anyone off.

Each year when the bus stopped in front of the church, the priest would run out as if he'd been waiting for us since our last visit. And each time he would perform the same routine—he'd shake his head, hug me tightly, and exclaim, "Olgetta—you are so grown up."

Olga was my sister. She was the firstborn child of my mother and father, but she was fourteen years older than me. There were no siblings between her birth and mine. She had lived in this village until she was seven years old when my father returned to reclaim my mother and was forced to take his daughter as well.

Once, when my mother was talking to one of her friends, I heard her say that my father had left her alone in Italy six weeks after my sister was born. He did not return for seven years. For the entire seven years she had no idea where my father had gone. She thought he might have gone to America, because he always talked about Washington D.C. and the cherry blossoms he swore bloomed in colors so bright you had to wear sunglasses to look at them, but she never found out, even after his return, exactly where he had been.

My mother said those had been hard years because he never sent any money to her. What he did send, every few months, were letters written by him, but mailed from Udine by someone my mother never knew.

"I'm watching you," the letters would say. "If I see you with another man, you and your daughter will be sorry."

The "your daughter" part stayed with me for a long time. I knew my sister had to be his child because out of all of us, my sister looked just like my father. It took me a few years to realize that my father's beef with her went way beyond any question of paternity. She might have been his by chance, but my brother and I were his by choice.

"No," my mother would say to the priest. "This is Denise. Olga is already grown with a baby on the way."

The priest would look disappointed, as if I were to blame for my sister's growing up and his ultimate aging.

My nona, not one to treat priests with much reverence, would leave us behind and begin walking down a dirt road toward a small enclave of houses grouped in a circle around a fountain. My mother's cousin Primo lived in one of the houses and even though my nona refused to speak to Primo's mother, her sister Teresa, the house had once been her family home. She was on her way to claim the best chair at the kitchen table.

My mother would linger at the church, speaking in Friulian to the priest. It was a dialect I despised because my mother only spoke it with my father, her sisters, and her mother. It sounded nothing like the Italian she spoke with everyone else in our lives.

"*Bing, bing,*" she would say softly to the priest.

"*Buono,*" I would say loudly to my brother. "She means *buono.*" When she spoke in Friulian, it felt like she was talking behind a closed door.

Once in a while, I would hear a catch in her voice and then my father's name. The priest would take her hands and they would pray. My mother gripped the hands of the priest tightly, as if holding him with all her strength would guarantee whatever she was praying for would come true. But I was suspicious of the priest. How much power could he have if he made the same mistake of confusing my sister and me every year?

At Primo's house, my brother and I would drink fizzy seltzer water from an old refrigerator, then chase chickens around the yard. Primo had never married and seemed nervous about having children in his house.

Boys named Primo were always the firstborn sons, but my mother told us that this Primo was actually the second Primo. The first one had been in the war and when he came home he fell in love with a woman from a neighboring village who was poor, even poorer than Primo's people. When his parents forbade the marriage, the first Primo said he respected their decision. A few days later Primo Number One came in from the field, ate his soup, took out a pistol, and shot himself in the head.

In English, so Primo Number Two couldn't understand, I asked my mother if the table they still sat around was the same table Primo Number One sat at when he ate his soup then pulled out his pistol.

"You ask too many questions," my mother said, but I noticed she didn't like to sit around the table either.

While my nona sat at that table looking at old pictures and talking about the land with Primo Number Two, my mother found ways to entertain us. She showed us the closet in the hallway where there had been a hole in the floor they'd used as a bathroom when they were children. She'd walk us to the fields to see the aging grapevines and to pet the goats.

Occasionally she'd walk around the circle of houses alone while my brother and I played in the fountain. I'd catch her looking toward the house where her childhood friend Concetta still lived. A few years back, when we'd gotten off the bus, there was Concetta waiting to board. My mother dropped her purse on the ground to hug her old friend, but in the blink of an eye my nona pulled my mother back and placed her palm on Concetta's chest, pushing her away. My mother reached down to pick up her purse and never looked back at Concetta. When I did, Concetta was crying.

"Why, Mom?" I asked as we followed Nona to the village. "Why wouldn't she let you talk to your friend?"

"When my father got black lung disease from the mines," my mother whispered, "Concetta told people he had tuberculosis. Everyone shunned our family. My mother has never forgiven her."

I loved my nona, but though the list of people she wouldn't forgive was long, it never seemed long enough to include my father. Whenever I tried to tell her how bad things were at home, she would turn her back to me and say, "*Non si sparla dei padre.*" We do not speak against the fathers.

After walking around the village, my mother took us far up the side of the hill so we could see the village from above. She promised to show us where she and her sisters had spent hours looking down at a house on the far side of the village, laughing at the antics of the people who lived there.

"One of the men had a little hat and he would take it off and tip his head to the wall," she said. "We laughed so hard, Maria Luisa almost pee-pee'd in her pants."

When we got to the ledge, my mother showed us how to lie on our stomachs and push ourselves forward to see down the side of the hill.

In the courtyard below were several men and women wearing what looked like hospital gowns. I figured out very quickly this was not a house, but a hospital for people with mental disorders.

"Mom," I said. "You were laughing at disabled people."

"I didn't know," she said, her face red with embarrassment. "They wore regular clothes back then. We didn't know."

For the first time, I began to question her judgment.

Texas

Sometimes the neighbors would call the police. Sometimes not. When my father woke at night and the gear in his head got stuck on rage, he would rip the pictures off the walls, toss the contents of drawers on the floor, and fling plants and coffee cups at the furniture. Someone in the house was always a bitch or an asshole, and none of us deserved all he did for us. By the time I was thirteen twice, I had a sense of what he'd given up for us—an education, the hope of a good job, his opportunity to fish alone by the ocean. I just wasn't sure what he was willing to do to have a chance at those things.

On a lucky night, my father would wander into the backyard screaming and yelling at the top of his lungs. My mom would spring into action, grabbing my brother and me and taking us to the car where she'd drive us to one of her friend's homes for the night.

On unlucky nights my father would storm through the house listening for anything that would call attention his way.

On the mornings after, we'd walk to the kitchen ignoring the debris in the house and on each other. Our house looked it had been ransacked by a burglar, but we sat next to the burglar at the table like it was just another day.

My mother served my father breakfast first. My brother and I sat quietly, waiting to see what he did with the plate. If he pushed it away, we braced ourselves like they taught us to do at school in the event of a tornado or an atom bomb. If he reached for the hot sauce to dump on his eggs, we waited for the jokes. He would make fun of my brother's bed head, or the dog struggling to smell our food, or someone on our street who didn't know their ass from their head. We'd laugh. Like it was all so funny.

Italy

After a few hours at Primo Number Two's house, another bus would come to take us to Gemona. Gemona was a larger city and there we would eat a late lunch before walking the few blocks to the Sanctuary of Saint Anthony. I always thought it was an awesome coincidence that we lived in a city in America named after my mother's favorite saint.

"I thought it was a sign," my mother said. "When we came to America, your father asked me if I wanted to move to Virginia or San Antonio. When I heard the name, I said San Antonio."

I wondered a lot about what life would have been like in Virginia.

My mother held my hand as we walked behind the newer, grander church toward the ancient ruins in the back. To get to the grotto of Saint Anthony, you first walked through a rock hallway—something like an ancient pedestrian tunnel. The smell of grass instantly became the smell of stone covered in age and smoke and the touch of thousands of fingers and hands.

A long line of people slowly shuffled single file through the tunnel, stopping often to read the notes of thanksgiving on the walls. These had been left to Sant'Antonio for miracles delivered. There were pictures taped to the notes as well. One picture was of a small boy without legs sitting on what looked like a broken-down tractor. "Thank you, Sant'Antonio for saving our son after he fell from the tractor and was run over." After a few dozen notes, I felt hot and sick to my stomach, overwhelmed by the intensity of the emotion stuck to the walls.

My mother never let go of my hand. The closer we got to the end of the tunnel, the stronger the scent of incense became. Once past the notes and pictures, we entered a small, dark room. Rows of hard wooden kneelers stretched across the brick floor. All the kneelers faced a white statue of Saint Anthony.

Candles burned in dozens of votive racks, and on hastily constructed shelves on the walls, and at the feet of Sant'Antonio. The statue looked on fire from all the shadows thrown by the lit candles. It seemed like all the air in the room was taken up by people and smoke and sorrow.

Once on my knees, I began poking holes in the stories from the pictures in the tunnel, faltering in my faith so quickly. Even though the boy who'd been run over by the tractor lived, he had no legs. I wasn't sure it was a full miracle. My mother would squeeze my hand, perhaps sensing I was about to bolt.

"Pay attention," she'd say. "Pray for your father. Pray for Sant'Antonio to make him change. Saint Anthony makes miracles happen."

And then I would. I would pray as hard as I could. My nona bobbed her head back and forth moving her lips and repeating *"il sangue di Gesù,"* the blood of Jesus, over and over. My mother pressed each bead of the rosary to her mouth. If I happened to catch my brother looking around or trying to read a hymnal, I'd pinch him. I was not about to let his lack of attention stand in the way of a miracle.

Texas

No matter how angry he was, my father always walked past my room. I had seen him break my brother's arm and kick my sister down the driveway. I'd seen him bite my mother on her breast. I was the only one my father never touched.

"Is he really my father?" I asked my mother.

"Don't be stupid," she said.

"He never hits me, Mom."

She sighed. "It's because you were born under *una buona stella*—how do you say—a lucky star."

Somehow, in the light of day, that made sense to me.

But in the middle of the night, I'd blame myself each time I heard a voice plead with him to stop. In the dark, on my stomach, I memorized every sound flesh can make when it is struck. I accepted that each punch or slap or hit was because of me—because I had faltered in my faith of Saint Anthony's miracles.

"Your mother doesn't love me as much as I love her," my father said, picking me up from my first youth group meeting after our return from Italy. I noticed a scratch under his chin from the night before. It was bleeding just a little. "She only loves your bitch sister."

I sat quietly in the truck. I was thirteen twice now. I'd learned that saying anything at times like these was like swearing you'd only throw one rock at a hornet's nest.

Italy

We were filled with a sense of hope when we left the sanctuary of Saint Anthony. We boarded the bus, headed back to Udine, and ate dinner at my nona's solid table made from the wood of the chestnut trees that grew in the forest near Ciseriis. Each time we made this pilgrimage my mother believed our rituals would be enough to make Sant'Antonio heal my father, make the impossible possible. And each time I wanted to believe it too.

———

Although everyone knows Saint Anthony as San Antonio de Padua, not everyone knows that he visited Gemona in 1227 to build a chapel honoring the Blessed Virgin Mary. Antonio never completed the building, but the ruins remained. The tunnel leading to the grotto was built from those ruins.

In 1976 a great earthquake demolished the tunnel and the grotto and the little chapel. I imagine all the notes, all the pictures, all the miracles were lost too.

We never returned to Gemona after 1975.

And there never was a miracle for my father.

MALOCCHIO (THE CURSE)

1988

Before I had a chance to say hello, my mother's voice shot through the phone. "You will never guess who called me."

"Who?"

"*Indovina*," she said. Guess.

I settled the phone between my shoulder and ear and waited.

"*Non puoi indovinare*," she said. You can't guess.

My interest was piqued, but only slightly. There was a remote possibility the call could somehow involve me—news about an old boyfriend or some gossip she'd heard about a friend—but more likely this was about her.

"No guesses," I said, looking around my apartment making sure it was clean, even though there was no way my mother could possibly see through the phone.

She sighed in the exasperated way only I could make her sigh. "You never want to have fun," she said. "Come on—guess."

I sighed back—loudly and dramatically. "Just tell me, Mom."

"Giuseppe," she said, in a voice usually reserved for repeating the Our Father at mass.

I'd heard stories about Giuseppe for so long now, it was like hearing that a character in a book was coming to dinner.

"Giuseppe? How did he find you?"

"Oh, now you want to ask questions," she said.

1978

At sixteen, I had my first boyfriend. He was a fellow high school thespian named Paul. Paul, older than me by a few critical years, was not as invested in the relationship as I was. I felt sure he was already planning a future where my name would be nothing more to him than an old listing in a playbill.

Over bowls of lukewarm queso and glasses of sweet tea, Paul told our theater friends about his plans to leave San Antonio the week after his high school graduation. As he spoke, his blue eyes looked clear and fresh, like he'd just taken a long swim in a cool pool. My eyes looked toward the ground, as if I'd lost something everyone else had given up finding. Our friends nodded, in awe of Paul's news. I tried not to give away how all of this was a surprise to me.

Back in my parent's driveway, I reached for the door handle.

"Wait," Paul said. "I want to tell you something."

I waited to hear how hard it would be for him to leave me. I waited for him to ask me to go to Europe with him. I'd have settled for an "I'm sorry. I couldn't tell you this earlier because it made me too sad." I took my hand off the door handle.

"Once I land in Italy, I'm taking a train to Genoa to visit my grandfather. He's been really sick, but imagine when he sees me. I haven't told anyone yet. I want it to be a surprise."

I nodded and looked out the side window. This was a guy who had never even planned a date night without my help. How had he done all of this on his own?

"You got nothing?" he said.

"Is this your grandfather who was in the circus?"

"Yep," he said.

"He's going to be really happy to see you."

I walked into the house, ran straight to my mother's bedroom, and began to cry.

"*Che c'e' che non va?*" she asked from the bathroom. What's wrong? Half her face was covered in Pond's cold cream.

"Paul's leaving in June and I'll never see him again. He made all these plans I didn't even know about. He told everyone tonight. Before he told me."

My mother nodded her head, ran to the bathroom, and returned with her face free of Pond's. She got into bed and covered us both with the bedspread. I put my head on her chest and listened to her heart beating calmly and gently, as if she'd wound it just for me.

"I know, I know," she said over and over, kissing the top of my head. "This feeling is terrible. Did you know I was in love with someone before I met your father? I was. And I never forgot him. We never forget the first hurt."

The sound of the word *we* made me feel like a woman for the first time in my life.

"His name was Giuseppe," she said.

1988

"He called you today?" I stretched out the phone cord so I could reach for my cigarettes on the coffee table. "Out of the blue?"

"Yes," my mother said. "Out of the blue. He called me on Monday, then I meeted him at Sizzler."

"Wait," I said, trying to light the cigarette as far away from the phone as I could. "*Meeted* him?" My mother's third language was English and her tenses were never quite right. "You *are* going to meet him or you *already did* meet him?"

"Yesterday," she said. "For lunch. Nadine came with me."

Nadine. That this was the friend my mother chose to accompany her to Sizzler bothered me. Nadine and my mother became friends in Europe when I was six weeks old. Years later, Nadine's husband and my father were both stationed in San Antonio, Texas.

Nadine was French in the way Brigitte Bardot was French. She was elegant and glamorous and a little dangerous. Hours of my life had been spent eavesdropping while my mother talked to Nadine about her newest lover. Nadine was married to the same man she had been married to for years, and she had three daughters, but Nadine was not tame like my mother and the rest of her friends. My mother was no Nadine.

"What did he want?" I asked, purposefully not saying the name Giuseppe. I exhaled the smoke from my cigarette while covering the phone.

"*Ascolta tua madre*," she said. Listen to your mother. "Don't smoke so much." And then, "He wants my mother to break the curse she put on him."

1978

In bed, with the lights off, I played with my mother's wedding ring, twisting it around and around her finger.

"Was he handsome? Giuseppe?" His name was a new taste on my tongue.

"Yes," she said, without hesitation. "He had dark hair and green eyes. I never met anyone with green eyes before that. And he was tall with big shoulders. I was so skinny that he could put me on top of one shoulder and carry me across the *torrente* in front of all his friends."

It was easy to picture my mother serving as arm candy for a nineteen-year-old boy to carry across a creek. She had been beautiful with long wavy hair and perfectly curved lips.

"*Ecco!*" she said. There you go! "You should have seen everyone laughing seeing me on top of his shoulder like a bird. Can you imagine if he tried to carry me today?"

I leaned onto my shoulder and looked at my mother. Her eyes were lit by the bathroom light. They were a light brown with so many specks of gold I used to think something had broken in them.

"You're still beautiful, Mom."

"*Come un porco*," she said, patting her stomach.

"You are not like a pig." She put my hand on her stomach moving it along the curve of her belly, as if that would prove her point.

"I see who I am," she said flatly. "No one will carry me on one shoulder again."

I twisted her wedding ring again. "Did Nona ever meet him?"

My nona was a large, imposing woman who could have easily carried my mother over a creek on her own broad shoulders. While we lived out our lives in San Antonio, my nona was a heavy presence from Italy, looming in the background like the Pope.

"He came to our house once," my mother said. "My parents were rude to him."

"Why?"

"My father didn't like that he was an American who might take me away. My mother hated him because she already knew he would break my heart."

"How did she know?"

"Because mothers know these things."

"Will Paul break my heart?"

"He already has," she whispered.

1988

"A curse?" I said, in a voice as loud as the one my mother had used when she first called me.

"*E' una lunga storia*," my mother said. It's a long story. "I told you Giuseppe wanted to marry me, *vero*? In those days the Americans made soldiers who were younger than twenty-one get permission from their parents to marry foreign girls. Giuseppe went to California to get his parents to sign the papers. He never came back for me, *ti ricordi*? I told you all this."

"I remember."

"What I didn't tell you was that I had a nervous breakdown when he didn't come back for me. I cried every day. I couldn't eat for months. I got skinnier and skinnier and then my hair started falling out. My mother was mad at Giuseppe. She told Maria Santo she was putting a curse on him and his family. Maria Santo had a daughter who worked at the army base and the daughter told a soldier at the base about the curse and when that soldier went back to America he contacted Giuseppe and told him about the curse."

"Why would Nona want to put a curse on his whole family?" I asked. "It seems like this was all Giuseppe's fault. Even if his parents didn't want to sign the papers, he could have told you the truth."

"Your nona had some idea that when Giuseppe got back to America his parents said no to the marriage because they thought our family was trash—poor people. All she could think was the Americans believed we were using him for money. The longer he stayed away, the sicker I got, and the madder my mother was. She wanted Giuseppe's family to suffer like we were suffering."

"But a curse? Does anyone really believe in curses?"

"*Di sicuro*," she said. Of course. "*Malocchio* is a powerful thing. You know how people want to find something to blame when things are not good. Giuseppe had bad luck after he returned to America. His brother lost his leg in a car accident, his father had a heart attack, and his sister's baby died right after it was born. Giuseppe decided all these things happened because of the curse. For a long time he didn't have the money to go back to Italy, but a few years ago, after more and more bad luck for him and his family, he flew to Italy to look for my mother. Nona had already moved to Udine, but he found Maria Santo still in our village. Because he wore a nice suit and gave her some cash, Maria Santo told him where my mother lived. He went to Udine to beg her to call off the curse."

"Did Nona remember him?"

"She said she knew him right away. He got on his knees and begged her for forgiveness. He brought her candy from the nicest store in Udine and a beautiful shawl from California."

"That was pretty brave of him to go find Nona. That took some nerve."

My nona stood as tall as most men. I imagined her opening the door dressed in her usual black outfit with eyes as dark as her clothing. This was a woman who walked out of her front door and snapped a branch from a tree every day before she walked down her street. She claimed the branch served as a switch to keep the flies away, but in truth she wielded it like a weapon so no one would get in her way on the sidewalk. I hoped Giuseppe had been scared when she opened the door.

"Did she put a curse on his family, Mom?"

"*Forse sì, forse no*," she said. Maybe yes, maybe no. "But it doesn't matter what is true—he *thinks* she put the curse. That's enough."

1978

"Mom," I said. "I'll never see Paul after he leaves. I just know it."

"You can't know that. It's too soon in your life to know what will or will not be. *Dal niente non viene niente.* From nothing comes nothing. Today, you know nothing about tomorrow."

The phone rang in the living room. My mother's leg jumped a little, like she wanted to run and answer it.

"It's probably Nadine," I said.

"She always calls to say good night. Sometimes we fall asleep while talking."

I laughed. I'd come home many nights to find my mother on the couch with the phone between a pillow and her ear, snoring. I snuggled closer to her. "I don't know how, but you always make me feel better, Mommy."

"Temporary," she said. "You feel better now, but it's going to hurt again tomorrow and the day after that and after that. But you are strong and beautiful and you have a good momma here to help you, *va bene*?"

"Yes," I said, feeling sleepy.

"You are a better daughter than I was," she said, looking up at the ceiling. "I understand the first boy—the first love. I take your feelings seriously. Okay? When I was hurt and crying, my mother called me *put-tana*. She said Giuseppe left because I was a whore."

"What?" I said. "Nona is so mean."

"It's true, she can be mean, but she can also be right. If I'd listened to her in the first place, I wouldn't have been so hurt when he left. I did bad things with Giuseppe. I let him have sex with me in the fields behind our house. After, he said he still loved me, but we had more nights in the field so what else was he going to say? He went to San Francisco and I never heard from him again. Not a card, not a letter, *niente*. Like I was no better than a whore."

We both stared at the ceiling. "I still believe he loved me in some way," my mother said. "But now that I have your brother, I understand how Giuseppe's mother felt. A poor Italian girl was trying to come to America by trapping her son."

"Wasn't Giuseppe's family Italian too?"

"Yes, but they were American first. His parents had never even been to Italy. They called him Joe. We called him Giuseppe. He said he liked it."

I had never considered the difference between an Italian-American and Italians before. All of my mother's friends had been born in Italy, except Nadine. They'd all married American soldiers. I hardly knew any Italian-Americans. Even Paul's parents had come from Italy.

"My mother said that because I gave him sex too soon, Giuseppe thought I was not good enough to be a wife. I guess she was right in a way. If he wanted to find me again, he would have—mother or not."

"How did Nona know you had sex with him?"

"I told her," my mother said. "I was always so stupid. I even told your father before I got serious with him."

"What?" I said, sitting up.

"I did. I thought he should know. *E'giusto*, no?"

"Well, sure. I mean I guess that's fair, Mom, but what did Dad do when you told him?"

"He was mad," she said. "He slapped me until I bled from my nose. When I went home with blood on my shirt, my mother turned her head from me and made the sign of the cross. *Colpa tua*. My fault."

"That is messed up, Mom. Dad hitting you was never your fault. Not now. Not then."

"Easy to say now," she said. "But I was young then. I didn't think anyone would take me after I had sex with someone else."

I kissed my mother's hand over and over, but kissing her hand reminded me of earlier that night when Paul had been unwrapping the plans that didn't include me. To get his attention I'd reached under the table and rubbed between his legs. He'd moved my hand away and continued talking.

When I walked to the bathroom, Paul followed me. As soon as the door closed, he locked it and grabbed me by the shoulders, slamming my back into the wall and into the bathroom hand dryer. While I was pinned by his body, he grabbed my breasts roughly.

"Is this what you want?" he said. "Is this the kind of attention you want from me?"

"Stop it," I said, trying to push him back. My shoulder was aching from the dryer vent.

"Don't act like that in front of people," Paul said, pushing me into the wall with each word. "You're better than that. You're not a stupid whore."

Paul left me in the bathroom with my back against the wall. I moved away from the dryer and tried to figure out how I felt about what just happened.

I was sixteen. I'd wanted attention from my boyfriend. I knew I wasn't a whore. I didn't need Paul to tell me that. But what I'd done was stupid. And embarrassing.

When my nona told my mother she was a whore, my father reinforced it with a slap. She had been young then too. And in love with Giuseppe. Would we both allow ourselves to be defined by others? Would I let myself be physically marked at the hands of a man too?

1988

"The curse was just an excuse," I said. "He went to Italy to find you. He wanted to see you."

"No," my mother said. Her practical nature was so annoying. I'd learned long ago never to ask my mother things like if an outfit made me look fat because she would answer, "Of course. When you are fat, you look fat." I called her insensitive. She said she was honest. We landed on practical. "All those years before, he could have found me if he tried. He went to Udine almost two years ago, but he just called me this week. He said he couldn't call before because he was in the middle of a divorce. He has had a lot of bad luck with women. He's been married and divorced four times. Can you imagine?"

"Stop," I said, lighting another cigarette, not sure what I should unpack first. "Two years? You've known for two years he was looking for you?"

"*Certo che no.* Of course not. Nona told me a few months ago when I went to Italy. She would never put something like that in a letter or say such a thing on the phone. Can you imagine if your father found out?"

I wasn't sure what to think of a family matriarch who could keep a secret like this for two years.

———

A few weeks earlier I had flown from Dallas to visit my mother after she returned from her trip to Italy. While she got ready for bed, I sat on the toilet and waited.

"Hey," I said, as she pulled her nightgown over her back. "What's this?" There was a bruise the size of piece of bread below her shoulder.

She shrugged.

"What happened?" In years past she might have kept her secret. She'd have told me she bumped into the wall, or something had fallen off the shelf and hit her, or she'd slipped getting out of the tub.

"*Cosa importa?*" she said, pulling her nightgown down. Why does it matter?

"It matters to me," I said. "What did he do?"

"The night I came back from Italy, your father was tired when he picked me up from the airport. The traffic was bad and then when we got home there was nothing for me to cook him for dinner. He was upset and hit me with the back of his shoe."

"Mom. You told that story all wrong. There was no reason for him to hit you—not that he was tired, not that the traffic was bad, not that there was no food."

She shrugged her shoulders. "I should have thought before I left to have a little something ready for when I got home. He was nice enough to let me go to Italy for six weeks. Your father works hard."

This was a version of the same conversation we would have forever. My father had an issue, he hit her. In her mind, if she had done one thing differently, she could have prevented the whole thing.

"You don't have to stay with him anymore," I said, over the sound of the toilet flushing so he couldn't hear us. "We're all out of the house. You can go."

"I can never go," she said. "You don't understand. If I ever leave, he will kill me. He will never let me be happy. Never."

"How do you know?"

"He told me years ago and he reminds me still today. If I leave, he will kill me. You've seen what he can do. So I am staying here and making the best of it."

"You never told me," I said.

"What could you do?"

———

"Did you hear me?" she said on the phone. I put my cigarette out and reached for another.

"Yes, I heard. Was he still handsome? Giuseppe?" I added his name as a gift to her after remembering the bruise on her shoulder.

"Yes. He is as tall as I remembered and he still has all his hair. It's gray now, but distinguished, like Ed McMahon."

I rolled my eyes. For some reason my mother thought Ed McMahon was the epitome of class.

"What did he think of you?"

"He said I needed to lose weight. He said I looked the same except I have a stomach."

"I don't like that."

"Eh," she said. "It might not be nice, but it's true."

"What did you do after he said that?"

"We were at the salad bar at Sizzler when he told me I shouldn't put dressing on my salad because I had the stomach. Well, that was it. There was no way I was going to let another man tell me what to do. So I took the white dressing that looks like glue—what do you call it?"

"Ranch."

"*Si*. Ranch. I took a big cup and poured it on my salad."

"You hate ranch dressing."

"I decided I hate people telling me what to do more than I hate ranch dressing."

I put my cigarette out and tried to cough to hide the weird hiccupping noise coming from my gut.

"Are you crying?" my mother asked.

"I'm proud of you."

"For putting dressing on my salad?"

"You stood up to him, Mom."

"Ah—but that's easy. I don't owe him anything," she said. "I will eat what I want in front of him."

"What did Nadine think of all this?"

"Right before she dropped us off at his hotel, she winked at me. She thought he was handsome."

"You went to a hotel with him?"

"*Allora, cosa ne pensate.*" What do you think? "He wanted to talk in private about the curse, so I went."

1978

The bathroom light was still on, so I looked to see if my mother was still awake. Her eyes were open and her breath soft.

"Mom?" I said. "I wasn't better than you. I had sex with Paul."

"I know you did," she said, turning on her side to face me. "I read your notes to Lisa."

I thought about what I might have said to Lisa in those notes. We had a habit, like most of the girls in my high school, of writing notes to each other during class, passing them to one another, and replying on the back or in the margins.

I hadn't imagined my mother to be the kind of parent to go poking through my notes, but at the same time, I understood the power of curiosity. Every time my parents left the house, I would dig through the drawers where they kept important documents wondering what new information I might find.

"Are you mad at me?" I asked.

"No," she said. "I wish you weren't so young, but I understand. You just have to be careful, you know?"

"Of course," I said. "I'm not stupid."

"Everyone is stupid sometimes," she said. "Are you sorry you did it?"

I was sorry tonight had happened. I was sorry I'd grabbed between Paul's legs. I was sorry about the bathroom. I was sorry I had taken the way he treated me.

I was also sorry I couldn't tell my mother the whole story. She had enough in her life to worry about.

"A little," I admitted. "But only because he's leaving anyway. I'm sad I'm not enough to keep him here."

"See?" my mother said. "That was a stupid thing you said. Paul is young. He wants to try on life. He knows you fit him, but everyone loves new clothes. It doesn't mean anything is wrong with the old ones."

"That is the dumbest thing I've ever heard, Mom."

"It might be dumb, but it's right. I would never tell you not to enjoy being with a boy. Just be careful. With your body and your heart. You are young and people make lots of mistakes when they are learning. Look how many accidents you had when you started to drive."

"Maybe Giuseppe made a mistake when he left you, Mom. He was young too."

"Maybe yes, but maybe no. There is a thin line between what we do and what we let happen."

We got quiet. My mother's breathing got louder. I thought about Paul and the bathroom and how I'd left feeling shamed. I'd let it happen to me. My shoulder throbbed and I figured there would be a bruise in a few days. When people asked me how it got there, what would I say?

I made a fist and held it against my forehead. I was not going to be my mother. I was never going to let anyone pin me against a wall again.

Without realizing it, I began building walls of my own.

1988

I wasn't sure what to say to my mother next. She had gone to a hotel with a man she had once loved. She was married to a man who abused her and threatened to kill her. How could she put herself in danger like this?

"What did you say to him about the curse?"

"I said I would tell my mother to break it off."

"And did you?"

"No. I'm not going to ask her if she put a curse. That would be rude."

She had been in his hotel room. All they did was talk about the curse?

"Listen," she said, before I could think. "Nadine took some pictures of me and Giuseppe at Sizzler. I want to mail them to you. Will you keep them so your father never sees them?"

"Sure," I said.

"Your sister will lose them or I would ask her."

"It's no big deal," I said. But it was such a big deal. If my father found out, what would he do? All of these years she had put her love into her children and now someone could take that away—either my father or Giuseppe. I felt like such an ass for wanting things to stay the way they were. We knew the rules—all of us. It made no sense to change things.

"Are you going to leave Daddy?" I never called him Daddy. A daddy was safe, like a certain tree during a game of tag. If my father was a tree, it was a Texas huisache, thorny, grown to hurt. Why had I called him Daddy now? Like a child.

"You know I can't."

"Would you if you could?"

"Yes," she said. "Giuseppe is so much fun. He likes to dance and drink wine and he enjoys having people around. We could have a full life together. That's all I ever wanted."

"Well, I'm glad you had fun then," I said. I'm not sure it was very kind. "Send me the pictures. I have to get ready for work now."

"*Va bene*. I love you," she said. She wanted to say more. I could feel the words waiting in the air like dust after you've polished wood.

I should have asked her how it felt to be back in the arms of a man she'd loved so much she had lost her hair because of him. I wish I'd asked her how often she'd thought of him over the years. But I didn't. I was too afraid to lose the only world I knew. It was all shit, but it was what I knew.

———

The pictures came in a box packed with the coffee-flavored candy my mother knew I loved and a leather wallet. When I looked at the pictures, I was surprised by how small my mother looked next to the tall man with broad shoulders. He held her as if he could still carry her across a stream with one arm. In another picture, they stood in front of the Sizzler bull with his arm around her waist. She leaned into him like she knew exactly where to go. They looked like a couple. They looked happy. They looked natural, like maybe it was meant to be.

2011

When I called my sister, she answered on the second ring.

"I'm so sad," I said.

"Why?" She yawned, as if she couldn't be less interested.

"Do you remember those pictures of Mom and Giuseppe? Water got into my garage and now they're ruined."

"Mom is dead," she said. "She won't care."

"But I do."

"When was the last time you looked at those pictures?"

I had never looked at the pictures after my mom mailed them to me. A few times, when my mother came to visit me, I'd given her the leather wallet and watched as she went to another room with them.

"Did Mom have an affair with Giuseppe?"

"Of course she did," my sister said. "Are you that naïve? I met him a few times too."

"She never told me." The sun went behind a cloud and I opened the blinds.

"Why would she tell you? She knew little Miss Perfect didn't want to know."

My sister hung up. I sat with the words she'd called me most of my life. Little Miss Perfect. It took until I was a teenager to realize this was meant as an insult. I thought it was good to do everything right. To keep from becoming like the rest of my family. Victims. Casualties. I followed all the rules in school, in the car, even returning things to stores if I'd been undercharged.

What looked like perfection was really an attempt to control chaos.

A friend of mine once overheard my sister calling me Little Miss Perfect and told me about the Mr. Men and Little Miss series of children's books by Roger Hargreaves. There is no Little Miss Perfect book, but Mr. Perfect is written like he's a perfect pill. He does everything right.

He is overly thoughtful of his friends and his society, only to be told off at the end of the book for having the fault of having no faults. My friend laughed at the end of the book, but it was a joke I missed. I couldn't see what Mr. Perfect had done wrong except be a little uptight. And, obviously, unlikable.

When my sister died, she left behind dozens of journals. Some of her comments about our family were cruel. Some were on the nose. I knew what I'd find when she wrote about me: "Thinks she's better than everyone. Thinks she's so perfect. Thinks her shit don't stink."

She was mostly right. But when you grow up in chaos, you aren't afforded too many mistakes if you want to survive.

When my mother was eighty, I took her to the grocery store one afternoon.

"Guess what?" I said. "I found a picture of your old house in Ciseriis on Google Earth. I'll show you later."

"Oh," she said. "You can do everything with that computer. Can you find my cousin Bruno in Belgium?"

"Where in Belgium, Mom?"

"I'm not sure."

"We can try later. Would you ever want to look for Giuseppe?" My father had been dead for three years.

"Giuseppe is probably dead," she said.

"What if he's not?"

"He would be my age. Eighty years old. What would we do?"

"Did things get better for his family after he thought your mother took away the curse?"

"He thought so, but the same things happened anyway. His mother died, his sister was in a bad accident, and he lost his job—that's life. It's normal for bad things to happen, curse or no curse."

"Did he ever tell you he was sorry he never came back to marry you, Mom?"

"I didn't ask," she said. "No answer would have made me happy. Think about it."

I put my hand on hers, imagining we were having a moment.

"You made me feel like my mother did when I told her I had sex with Giuseppe," she said softly in Italian. "Like I was nothing but a whore."

"What?"

"Nothing," she said. "I was just thinking out loud."

I let us both pretend I hadn't heard her.

MY MOTHER TELLS ME

My mother tells me she had no idea a man could be as mean as my father. Her own father, she says, was like a saint.

"My father never raised his voice, never hit any of us, never tore the house apart."

"That qualifies him for sainthood?" I ask my mother. "Isn't that what normal fathers don't do?"

She ignores me, hands over another piece of broken glass. I place it in the trash bag, tie a knot at the top, and reach for a new bag.

———

In the middle of the night, my father, stumbling over his own darkness, broke every breakable object in the living room.

This is not an unusual occurrence.

"Your father has a lot on his mind," my mother tells me as we survey the living room together.

The space contains everything you need to live comfortably in a house: a couch, a recliner, a coffee table. All the superfluous items, the things that enhance a room, are on the floor, or splattered on the wall, or tossed in a corner like a pile of leaves.

The room looks like the set from a television show after a fight scene.

"Where is he?"

"Sleeping," she says, calmly. "Let's clean before he wakes up."

———

"*Aspetta*," she says now as I shake the new trash bag open. Wait. "I need to sit for a minute."

She rubs the base of her spine with the palm of her hand. I guide her into a chair, take a pillow from the couch, place it behind her back. She is getting old. Too old to spend weekends shopping at garage sales for more objects my father will destroy.

In the kitchen, I find a Sprite, a couple of glasses, and some Tylenol. I sit next to her at the dining room table in chairs that do not face the living room.

"Your father works hard," my mother says. "Sometimes he wakes up angry."

"You never saw your father angry?" I ask, ignoring the familiar excuse she uses for my father's behavior.

My mother closes her eyes tight, as if shutting every door in front of her might open a back door to a memory. "Just one time," she says, opening her eyes. "When I was twelve. The war had started, and we left France because they were bombing the coalmines where my father worked. We moved back to Italy, to his family village, and we were eating dinner together at the kitchen table in Ciseriis. It was just the three of us then. Both of my sisters were gone. Armida was working in Switzerland. Maria Luisa was married. She was the oldest. I was the baby, remember?"

My mother likes to remind me she was the baby of the family. Babies are blameless, after all.

"My poor sisters. When Maria Luisa was fourteen, my parents sent her from France to work for a family in Udine. And when Armida was fourteen, it was 1939. People were starting to talk about the war so they sent her to Switzerland to work. Many of the poor families, like mine, sent their children away. I was too young."

"The baby," I say.

"Yes," my mother smiles, sips her Sprite. "So there we were, eating dinner. My mother started telling us about a lady whose house she'd cleaned that day. When my mother took the sheets off the clothesline, the lady said they smelled funny. My mother was being loud, because she was acting like the lady. I was laughing so hard. Suddenly my father slapped his hand on the table and said, 'Enough, Carolina. *Sta zitto*.'" Shut up.

"What did your mother do?"

"She shut up. We both did. My father had never raised his voice to any of us before and we were surprised."

My mother busies herself arranging the salt and pepper shakers just so in the middle of the dining room table, then brushes invisible crumbs into her hand. Her house is always so clean. It is something she can control.

"That was it? That was the one time he got mad?"

"No," my mother says, taking in a breath, putting on a smile that looks like high heels, hard to wear. "After my father yelled, my mother got up from the table and went into the kitchen. I heard a match being struck so I thought she was smoking her one cigarette of the day. But soon she came back with a cup in her hand. It was full of hot polenta that had been heating on the stove. She threw it on the back of my father's head."

"Are you serious? That's crazy, Mom. Was he burned?"

"I don't remember that part," my mother says. "He jumped up, my father, and ran to the kitchen. I sat at the table waiting to see what my mother would do next. All she did was pull out her chair and sit. When my father came back from the kitchen, he had a wet towel around his shoulders.

"'I don't like this table,' my mother told my father. 'The marble is too cold for my arms.'

"'Carolina,' my father said, 'this table will stay in our house until I die, then you can make it my tombstone.' And you know what, after he died, my mother sent the table to a stone cutter and turned it into my father's headstone."

"Wait a sec. I don't get it, Mom. Your father was so good he was like a saint, then all of a sudden, out of the blue, he yells at your mother, she tries to hurt him, and they argue about the kitchen table?"

"It was a marble table," my mother says, as if that explains the argument. "My mother was right; it was cold. But yes, it happened, just like that."

"That was the one time you saw him angry?"

"There is more, but it's part of the same story," my mother says. "So it counts as the same anger, yes?"

She waits for me to nod as if my answer is like one of those books where you can choose the direction of a story.

I nod.

"The next morning we were back at the table finishing breakfast when the door opened and Maria Luisa walked in. I was happy to see her, but when I ran to hug her, she pushed me away. I could see she was hurt. Her eye was red and bruised around the outside. I wondered if someone had thrown a ball at her face. Around her collar, her dress was ripped, like someone pulled her from behind. She held the material together tightly, as if it were the only thing keeping her inside her skin.

"'Valencia,' my mother said to me, 'go outside. Look for the cat. See if she had her kittens. Go.'

"I walked to the little shed behind our house. The cat did have kittens and I was so excited I forgot there was anything happening in the house. But soon, I heard Maria Luisa screaming. I peeked out of the small window at the top of the shed. My father had Maria Luisa by the hair and was pulling her like she was an animal to the part of the yard where the chickens lived."

"Mom," I say. "I think I'm missing some backstory. Was Maria Luisa in trouble?"

My mother stands up, takes her glass into the kitchen. She continues her story from the doorway. "I never told you about Maria Luisa, did I? I have to or the story makes no sense. When my sister was working in Udine, she had trouble with the man who was her boss. One night she ran away from the house where she worked. There she was, on the streets of the city with no way to contact our family, and no money to leave. My sister got hungry, of course, so she stole some food from a street cart and got caught. They threw her in jail and she had no way to pay to get out."

"Your sister was in jail at fourteen?"

"She was sixteen by then," my mother says. "But they kept her in jail like she was a common thief."

"What problems did she have with the man?"

"My sister said he was touching her. Years later she told me she ran away because he got her pregnant. She lost the baby while she was in jail. Can you imagine?"

I'd always imagined my Zia Luisa darker than her sisters, but I figured it was because of her thick black hair and deep brown eyes. Now I know it was the past that shadowed her.

"In jail, there was a man who came around every week to visit his cousin in the cell next to your zia. That was your zio Aderke."

"He hit on her while she was in jail?"

"Aderke? Don't be stupid. Back then they didn't have visiting areas. Aderke would take a stool and sit outside the bars to talk to his cousin. My sister was next to them. Eventually, to be nice, Aderke brought Maria Luisa grapes and cookies, and they started talking. He told her his wife had died a year before and left him with a seven-year-old daughter. One day he asked my sister if she wanted help getting out of jail. He told her he could give her a job taking care of the little girl."

"She didn't have much choice but to say yes, Mom."

"Maybe not. But Aderke had a nice place to live where she would have food and earn a little money. My sister said yes. The only problem was they would only release her to her family or a husband, so they got married."

"She was sixteen. How old was he?"

"Oh, who knows? Somewhere in his forties," my mother says. "Eventually she came to love him. He was handsome even if he was older."

"This is the saddest story ever," I say. I think back to the last time I saw Zio Aderke. I picture him standing over the kitchen sink with his dark black hair, hard, shiny shoes, and cruel frown sucking an uncooked egg out of a tiny hole he'd poked in the top with a knife. I remember shuddering. I shudder now. When my zia died at fifty-two years old, he must have been in his early eighties. He got two for one with her: someone who took care of his daughter when she was young and him when he was old. Did anyone ever take care of Maria Luisa?

"Why are we talking about my sister?" my mother asks.

"You were telling me the one time your father got mad. When your sister came to your house with a black eye."

"Okay," my mother sits at the table. "Apparently, the day before Maria Luisa came to our house, my father ran into someone in town who told him that my sister had been in jail. She never told my parents that story. We'd just moved back from France, remember? My father was mad because he thought she brought shame to our family while we were gone, so he went to look for her and they got into a big argument.

That morning when Maria Luisa came to the house, it was to beg my father's forgiveness, but he was still too mad to listen. As soon as my sister opened her mouth, my father pulled her toward the buckets where the chickens drank. He forced her to her knees and grabbed her hair again. I watched him push her face into the bucket, into the dirty water, again and again until my mother ran over with a big piece of wood and hit my father across his shoulders."

"Who hit her in the eye before she came to the house, Mom?"

"I don't know. I never asked."

My mother and I face each other like we ran a great distance and need a rest.

"So there," my mother tells me. "Now you know the one time I saw my father mad."

"Did he and Zia Luisa talk again?"

"Oh sure," my mother says. "In Italy we say, *La famiglia è la patria del cuore.*" Family is where the heart is. She bends and kisses my head, then faces the living room and the rest of the mess we have to clean up.

I pick up broken pieces of frames and bowls and figurines and wonder if that moment of anger from her father is when she learned to swallow hard? Did it happen sitting at the cold table hearing the near-saint yell? Or was it in the little shed watching her oldest sister nearly drown in a bucket of dirty water because she'd lied to protect a family who sent her away at fourteen? Was that one escape from sainthood how my mother learned to excuse my father's torture of our family by saying he was tired, worried, sick?

"We're almost done," my mother says, turning to look at the living room. I follow her eyes. The couch is full of pillows. My mother calls it elegant. I'm amazed to see it that way as well.

"Mom?" I ask, "Did it bother you that your father might have killed your sister?"

"Oh you," she says. "So dramatic. My father was a wonderful man, ask your cousin. He just had a bad moment. But nothing happened really."

I throw a few pieces of pottery in the trash bag. The living room is finally clean, stripped of all color, all debris, anything decorative. When my mother moved to the United States from Italy, she brought nothing personal with her. There were no vases from our childhood home or picture frames or collectables. She left everything of value behind, where it was safe.

Tomorrow and the day after she will circle all the garage sales in the newspaper and then one by one walk through other people's lives to buy more objects that fit her definition of elegance. By next weekend we might sit in this very room with our father pretending everything in here is the same.

My mother scans the living room one more time and tells me, "I said my father was *close* to a saint, not that he *was* a saint. I know the difference."

I believe she does.

Seconda Parte: Buon Sangue Non Mente

PART TWO: GOOD BLOOD DOESN'T LIE

BETRAYED BY BLOOD

In 1973, the Squirrel Cage was just another scummy go-go bar on a street filled with businesses that paired well with scummy go-go bars. It's gone now, of course, replaced by an aboveground pool company—almost an elbow-to-the ribs attempt at baptismal humor.

The Squirrel Cage sat at the crossroads of Austin Highway and Walzem Road in San Antonio, Texas. In the distance, like a siren's song, was Interstate 35 luring cars north to Austin. I was thirteen then, living with my family in subsidized housing a very short distance from the Squirrel Cage. When I told adults where I lived, they looked away.

There were two playgrounds at the Austin Arms Apartments. One was for real kids—the ones who wanted to swing and teeter-totter and scream a lot; the other was the hangout for older kids, the ones who sat on the swings, lounged on the monkey bars, and whispered plans for future trouble.

My "because of proximity" best friend was a thirteen-year-old named Liz who stood nearly six feet tall. Her mother ran promotions at a local radio station. Liz always gave me inside information, like times to call in to a radio show so I could win prizes, but I never made any of those calls. When I saw her mom coming home from work wearing blouses with built-in bows at the neck, I couldn't see a woman who would jeopardize her job to help a preteen cheat a contest.

"You know so little about the world," Liz told me over and over. "Winners only win because they know people."

The older boys at the playground were probably not considered winners by Liz, but they knew a lot about how our small world worked. I listened while they talked about things like the icehouse on the corner where you could pay an extra fifty cents to get a six pack of beer without showing any ID. Judging from the number of beer cans littering the sides of the playground, I believed the story.

"You can also say you're getting cigarettes for your mom and they'll let you buy them," Kenny, a regular on the playground, said to a new kid I didn't know. Kenny's hair was so blond it was closer to white than yellow. People said his father was in prison for stabbing a truck driver in Fort Worth. Liz whispered about the knife collection Kenny had in his room, but that information made Kenny seem more sad than dangerous.

"Where is this place?" the new kid asked.

"Right across from the Squirrel Cage," Liz said. "On the other side of Walzem. Marty's Ice House."

The new kid nodded silently.

"Naked girls dance at the Squirrel Cage," Kenny whispered like he was giving up an answer to a test in school. "They dance in gold cages."

"Cages? Like birdcages?" Liz asked. She walked nearer to Kenny, making him shield his eyes from the sun as he looked up at her.

"Sure," Kenny said. "They hang the cages from the ceiling so everything shakes real good when they dance." He gyrated his hips and cupped his pecs. His tongue stuck out the side of his mouth as he shook.

The new boy laughed.

Liz rolled her eyes and walked away. "You don't know anything."

"I do too."

"Well, I know the girls aren't all the way naked," Liz said, looking at me as if we'd won *Jeopardy!* I went up a rung on the monkey bars. Liz could come across like a know-it-all sometimes.

"They got these little star things over their nips," Kenny said. "And go-go boots. Otherwise, they are naked." He paused, waiting to throw out his trump card. "My brother works there."

"He does?" I said.

"Is he in a cage too?" Liz laughed.

"Nah, but he could probably get *you* a job there," Kenny said, staring at my breasts. From my perch on the monkey bars, I crossed my legs.

The next week I went to Solo Serve with my mom so she could buy some new tops for summer. I waited until she went into the dressing room to try on clothes, then I walked to the shoe department. There was an entire rack devoted to go-go boots. I picked up a pair of shiny white boots and hid behind the coats to try them on. The boots were a cheap plastic, not leather at all, and smelled odd. Before I had the second boot zipped, my first leg began to sweat. Still, when I stood up and felt the silky material reach over the top of my knee like an unfamiliar hand, I stuck out my chest and sucked in my stomach.

Before I walked back to the dressing room, I stuffed the boots behind the men's work shoes hoping they'd stay hidden until I could figure out a way to buy them.

———

That night, my brother and I sat in the bedroom we shared listening to my mother plead with my father to calm down. They were in their bedroom with their door shut, which was never a good sign. Occasionally we heard a slap or a fall or a sharp cry. We didn't look at each other though, only at the Mickey Mouse rug beneath our feet. Our mother found the rug at a garage sale. She was always looking for ways to make our room look like the kind of room American kids would have. The Mickey on our rug was dancing in a tux and tails. He had a magic wand in his hand.

When I got out of bed, I always tried to step hard on the wand. For me, the rug was a reminder of all we would never be—the kind of kids who could believe in magic.

When their bedroom door finally opened, my mother came straight into our room. She was wearing a light blue robe. There were drops of blood around her collar, like she had sewn tiny roses around the neckline. Her right eye was already swollen.

"Let's go," she said, reaching for my brother's hand. He was nine and skinny, like something that could easily be broken in a move.

"Now," my mother said looking at me and pulling my brother toward the door. I followed.

The three of us ran down the two flights of stairs in harmony, as if we had trained for this event. When we pushed open the hall door, a neighbor opened her door, then quickly shut it. Outside, the cool air surprised me. My pajamas were light cotton. My brother had on short pajama bottoms and tube socks with green stripes. I was barefoot. It had been warm when we dressed for bed.

"Hurry," my mother said. "*Andiamo*," she said, as if those words were magic carpets that might make us move faster.

I tried to run without stepping on loose rocks or tabs from soda cans. Once we ran past the porch lights, I was glad for the dark so I wouldn't see what my feet were headed for.

I followed my mother's robe as she ran toward Austin Highway. When we got to the highway, she abruptly stopped and held her arms out to each side like a human cross. It was as if we stood on a precipice. The wind and noise from the cars sounded like an ocean far below us. My mother looked to her right, toward Austin and the Squirrel Cage, then ran to the left down the side of the busy road. She wore thin slippers and hobbled occasionally when her foot stepped on something sharp. She was not used to hot summer days and bare feet like we kids were.

We ran past tattoo parlors and bars and motels that seemed abandoned, but weren't. I finally saw the shopping center where my mother must have known she'd find a phone booth and safety. The Piggly Wiggly was already closed for the night, but inside the store employees were sweeping up and stocking shelves. I looked at the three of us and wondered if someone would call the cops. No one did.

My mother picked up the pay phone and dialed 0 for the operator. "I want to make a collect call," she said, giving the operator a number. "Marie," she said a few seconds later. "*Ho bisogno di aiuto*." I need help.

While we waited for Marie's husband Carlo to arrive, my mother went into mother mode. She found a planter box beneath a bright light with a wide ledge where we could sit out of the wind and get off our feet.

"It's going to be okay," she said, checking the bottoms of our feet. "Marie has milk for you and then we'll all go to bed. Tomorrow will be a better day." My mother's bottom lip was cracked, but the blood had dried a strange orange color.

It didn't take long for Carlo to arrive. He was a short, chubby Sicilian man with a thick head of hair he would keep well into his eighties.

"Valli," he said, hugging my mom. "Let's go, huh. Hi kids. Go ahead and get in the car." We slid off the planter and into his massive Cadillac.

As Carlo drove toward his house, I looked out the window and watched the neighborhood change, like I was a character in one of those movies where people's fortunes rapidly shift. As we crossed under Interstate 35, lighted coffee shops began to appear along with gas stations and restaurants and fancy furniture stores. When we got to the corner full of churches, I knew we were almost there.

This wasn't our first late-night visit to the Presti house. It wouldn't be the last. In the driveway, I saw the curtains in the front window open a bit.

We walked to the front door and Marie opened it wide. "*Entrate*," she said, leading us all gently by the shoulder, like refugees you see on the news at night. Come in, come in.

"Hey," I heard from down the hallway. I followed the voice and went into Nina's room. She was two years older than I was, beautiful and thin with a car she couldn't even drive yet waiting for her in the garage. "Same old same old?"

"Yep," I said.

Nina sat back in her canopy bed and patted the other side. The whole room was white and lavender and gold, like something I figured French aristocrats set up for their daughters. "So what's new?" she asked.

"I tried on some go-go boots the other day."

"What?" she said, stopping in mid-yawn. "Where?"

"Solo Serve. My mom was in the dressing room. Over the knee," I said, showing her where the boots had hit my thigh.

"Heels?"

"No," I said, suddenly disappointed in my choice. "I mean, little block ones. I guess that's easier to dance in, right?"

"At the Squirrel Cage! Those boots are the first part of the job interview. Boots? Check. Boobs? Check. You're hired!"

We laughed, then talked about some friends we knew until she fell asleep. It was good to feel normal, like this was any other sleepover with a friend. I had known Nina my whole life. Our mothers met in Europe when we were babies. Both husbands joined the military and ended up in San Antonio. Even though Carlo was an officer and my father was not, we never talked about that difference, or any of the other ones.

While Nina slept, I planned. I figured if I babysat every weekend for a month, I could buy the go-go boots. My breasts were already larger than most girls my age. Maybe, with makeup, I could get a job at the Squirrel Cage. Maybe I could make enough money we could leave my father behind.

In Nina's bathroom, I took off my pajama top and found some Band-Aids in the medicine cabinet. I taped my nipples and shook my body up and down and side to side. Some good shaking was going on beneath the Band-Aids.

Taking them off was a different matter. When the adhesive ripped away from the tender area around my nipples, tears sprang to my eyes. I ran a washcloth under cold water and held it to my breasts to stop the pain. I knew so little about my own body, but I had big plans for it anyway.

The next morning, Carlo drove us home. My brother and I got ready for school. My mother cooked breakfast. Their bedroom door stayed shut.

It wasn't easy to concentrate in class that day. During lunch I took my sandwich to the library, ate it in the bathroom, then grabbed a study table and planned. I wrote down the following:

Money:	+ $32.00	saved in the bank
	+ $40.00	possible babysitting money for weekends through March
	$29.99	boots
	$40.00?	gun

In the light of day, I'd realized that getting a job wasn't going to be enough to save us. Over the years, I'd heard my father threaten to kill my mother if she ever left him. Sometimes he even said he'd kill us kids first, then leave her alive so she would have to live knowing we were dead because of her. There was no simple getting away from him. We would live in fear as long as he was alive.

I was willing to fix that.

My dad worked all night delivering bundles of newspapers to boys on bicycles so they could deliver papers to their smaller routes. When he came home, he slept on the couch almost all afternoon. If I could get a gun, I would come home from school while he was asleep and solve all our problems.

After he died, I would go to school during the day and work at the Squirrel Cage at night to help with bills. We would be a happy family then. My mother was still beautiful. What if she met a nice man who could care for us all? There would be no more late-night trips to the Prestis', no more neighbors calling the police, no more sleeping on my stomach so I wouldn't see it coming.

I felt like a hero in the making.

This plan consumed my thoughts for months. I fixated on how to make sure my father would be asleep when I walked in the door. Like a director, I blocked and reblocked the scene over and over imagining every possible pitfall. I wanted to avoid hitting a noisy step and causing the dog across the hall to bark. If I dropped the gun or my book bag or my keys, or mistimed the departure of the postman who always said hello in a too-loud voice that echoed in the hallway, my father might wake up. I needed my father soundly asleep when I walked through the door because I knew if he looked at me, I couldn't kill him.

I spent weekends at the public library researching social security benefits my mother and brother could get from my dead father. I wasn't sure I would get them too, since I was the one who killed him, but I had the phantom job at the Squirrel Cage anyway. I read about trials where children killed their abusers and were set free or placed in detention centers for a short time. I learned what I was doing was called *parricide*, the killing of a parent, and I hoped the outcome would not be living in a detention center, but a conviction of manslaughter, probation, and the right to live at home.

I kept notebooks filled with details of the plan. The notebook was my confessor because there was no one else to talk through my plan with. There were no conversations about things like abuse on TV or on the playground or in our kitchen. After a night of beatings, my mother would tell us that my father had just been tired, or worked too hard, or didn't feel good.

"Everyone has something," she told me one night. I was suspicious of everyone after that.

I babysat every weekend in March and ended up with $47.00. One of the mothers, each of the two times I babysat her kids, brought a different man home with her. "Shhh," she said, holding her index finger across her mouth. "He'll be gone before they wake up." She gave me an extra two dollars both nights.

One of the couples lived in a house painted yellow with a baby who was asleep when they left and still asleep when they returned. They left a *Playboy* in the hall bathroom. I used toilet paper to put it in the bottom drawer of the bathroom cabinet. They tipped me three dollars.

I called my mother once I was alone in the houses and told her how the women looked when they left the house and what kind of furniture they had and how clean their kitchens were. It was nice to get lost in someone else's life.

―――――

"Hey, Kenny," I said, surprising him at school one day when Liz was not around. "Where do people buy guns?"

Kenny shrugged his shoulders. "Why are you asking me?"

I raised my eyebrows.

"The flea market maybe?" Kenny said.

"Ask your brother for me, okay? Also, ask him how I can get a job at the Squirrel Cage."

"Sure," Kenny said, but he looked at me like I had once given him a gift and was taking it back. "My brother doesn't even have a gun."

"Just ask him, okay?"

Kenny nodded.

―――――

In June, my father surprised us by buying a house. My mother was happier than I'd ever seen her. "I told your father I wanted a house before I turned fifty," she said, as if she had stumbled upon a winning lottery ticket. "And here it is. I can't wait to invite Marie over for coffee."

My plan died there. If I killed my father now, there would be no

58

house. I would no longer be the hero. I let go of the gun, the boots, and the Squirrel Cage and concentrated on the new house and the new version of our family instead.

———

In September of 1973, in the living room of our new house, I watched the season two opening episode of the TV sitcom *Maude*. The show began with lots of references to drinking. The night before, a drunk Walter made obscene phone calls to Maude's mother, slow danced with his friend Arthur, and fell asleep on the living room floor. The audience laughed as each exploit was recalled. Boys will be boys. The next morning, somewhat shamed by the night before, Walter and Arthur decide to stop drinking. By lunchtime, Walter is already spiking his Shirley Temple. By dinnertime, Walter is so drunk he ruins his nine-year-old grandson's birthday cake. The whole time, laughter from the audience. Drunk is funny. Bea Arthur is funny. Hey, she's drunk too. Then things turn dark. Maude tells Walter he's "different" when he drinks. Walter tells Maude he drinks because all he sees when he looks into her eyes is how much she resents him.

Then he hits her.

In the face.

Hard.

The laughter stops. You can hear the audience's collective intake of breath. Walter looks appropriately shocked by his own actions.

Then he cries.

"You didn't hurt me," Maude assures Walter. *MAUDE* ASSURES *WALTER*. Her tag line on the show was, "God will get you for that, Walter," but she didn't utter it this time.

In the morning, Maude sits at the breakfast table with a cup of coffee and a black eye. She tells her daughter she walked into a chocolate donut. Laughter again.

Until that episode aired, I'd never seen a man hit a woman anywhere but in my own home. It felt like a shameful secret we just lived with. And Maude playing it off reinforced what my mother taught us—don't let people know, pretend it's all okay, be better so we look better.

The episode wasn't a total waste though. It taught me to blame everything on alcohol. Though I never saw my father take one sip of alcohol in my entire life, from then on when neighbors called the police, I had a ready excuse. Thank you, Maude.

We were in our house for a year when I heard my parents arguing through my closed bedroom door. The fight was unusual because it was daytime and because things had been calmer since we'd moved into the house. I walked toward the kitchen and passed my brother sitting on the floor of his bedroom playing with G.I. Joes.

"What's up?"

He shrugged his shoulders, not taking his eyes off the action on his floor.

In the kitchen, my father had my mother by the throat. Her head was against the brick wall. The pistachio-colored bricks were her favorite part of the new house. I saw blood on her forehead and on the brick.

"Stop it," I screamed. "Stop it, you asshole."

When he turned toward me, I slugged him, close-fisted, on the mouth. A tooth must have hit his lip and the blood began to flow. He reached up to his face, looked at his hand, then at me.

His eyes said he'd been betrayed.

Betrayed by blood.

While he walked to the bathroom, my mother yelled for my brother. We all ran to the garage, into the car, and back to the Prestis'. None of us said a word until we hit Austin Highway.

At the stoplight, my mother sighed. "Tomorrow you'll tell him you're sorry."

"No way," I said. "I'm not sorry."

"You hit him," she said. "What did he do to you?"

I'm guessing there is a feeling people get when they realize they are completely alone in the world. It feels like you are drowning from the inside out. The instinct to hold your breath is almost involuntary, like a gift to keep you from speaking or crying out or taking in something that will prevent you from ever opening your mouth again.

We passed the Squirrel Cage and I remembered how that place had once been the church I sent my prayers to. Now I knew that if I had gotten a gun, if I had killed my father, my mother wouldn't have taken my side. I imagined her in court, talking to the judge, "He never did anything to her. He was a good father."

I was the one betrayed by blood.

When we returned to the house the next day, the door to my bedroom had been removed. I knew it was part of my punishment, but I couldn't figure out how. Over the years it became clearer. I could no longer try on clothes for the school week posing in front of the mirror that once hung on the back of my door. I couldn't dance to records and pretend I was in a Broadway musical, or read plays out loud, acting out each of the parts, or shut out the noise when things got bad.

For the next five years, my father refused to speak to me. All through high school, I was into theater. He never saw one of my productions, not even when we won the University Interscholastic League's One-Act Play Contest. He missed my high school graduation, seeing me go to proms, and taking part in any plans for the scholarships I received to colleges.

For five years we never ate a meal at the same table, watched TV in the same room, or looked at old family photos. My brother and mother and father still did all those things together. I was the excommunicated one.

At least once a week my mother would come to me like a temptress in a fairy tale: "Just say you're sorry. Then he will talk to you."

"I'm not sorry."

"You don't have to be sorry. Just say it. Then we can go back to normal."

There is a long list of things I am not proud of in my life, but not giving in to my father is not on that list.

———

At the end of my freshman year in college, my mother's sister and her husband arrived from Switzerland to stay with my parents for the summer and take a tour of the USA. I loved Zia Armida. She'd confided in me that she'd left her home at fourteen to become a maid for a family in Switzerland just so she wouldn't have to stay in Italy and marry an Italian man. In her mid-twenties, she met my zio Jean-Pierre, a native of the French part of Switzerland. He was a watch engineer and mayor of their small town. My father adored my zio. He called him his brother.

I was living with my friend Lisa for the summer. Her parents went to the beach every June and July, so living together was a good solution for both of us.

When I drove up to my parents' house, my zia was sitting on the front porch wrapped in a blanket.

"*Fa cosi freddo dentro*," she said to me. It's so cold inside. It was June in San Antonio. It had been hot for so long, we'd already stopped complaining.

"They don't like air conditioning," my father said to me. And just like that, we began to talk. I knew it was so he could save face in front of my zio, but I played along.

My mother hugged me when my father went back into the house.

"See? Everything is good now."

"Mom, everything is the same. We're just talking again."

"Good," she said. "That's how it should be with family. Forgive and forget."

My father finally got too old to be mean, then he died.

My mother lived another three years after his death.

As a child, her family left Italy and moved to France after her father found work in the coal mines. When she was twelve, and World War II began to escalate, they fled France, where the coal mines were being bombed, to return to Italy, only to find Russian armies occupying their family land. My mother went through puberty hungry and scared, but entered adulthood strong and cunning.

She picked me as the child to count on because she knew how to survive. When the chips were down, when my family was in crisis, I contacted doctors, lawyers, bankers. I put all the pieces together for all the cracked eggs after all the big falls.

I also became bitter and resentful and keenly aware of how much my mother seemed to love best the ones who hurt her the most. But, like most things in life, we adapt to our roles.

When I talk about my mother's final days, I talk about her strength and courage. I tell the story of how my husband held her face after the nurse gave her what I always suspected was a larger-than-usual dose of morphine and said, "Mom, if you can, come back and let us know you're okay." She nodded and expelled her last breath. It was a breath of force and finality. She'd made up her mind to go.

A few years after my mother died, my sister died as well. Her kids struggled with their own grief and guilt. They also had to turn to me for help. When my niece texted asking for $350.00, I told my husband I was going to say no.

"We just gave her money a few weeks ago," I said. "And she never thanked us. She never calls to check on us either. I'm done."

Before I could finish my text to her, the postman rang the doorbell and handed my husband a certified letter from State Farm Insurance.

It was that dramatic.

In the envelope was a check for $349.83. The refund was from a six-year-old audit they had completed of my mother's insurance policy.

I texted my niece and told her she could have the $350.00. Could there have been a clearer sign from my mother that she wanted to help my niece?

———

Later that day, I drove to Brackenridge Park. I sat on a concrete ledge facing the green water of the San Antonio River and watched the ugly hybrid ducks swim by. Across the river families played loud music and sat on blankets in the grass. It seemed appropriate I was on the other side of the divide.

"Sorry," a woman said as her dog began licking my leg. She grabbed his leash and pulled the dog away. "Do you teach at Northwest Vista College?"

I nodded.

"Miss Tolan?"

I nodded again.

"I had you for Comp II," she said. "About eight years ago. I loved your class."

I said I remembered her, but I didn't.

What I did remember was going to the grocery store with my mother a few months before she died. We'd run into an Italian woman I had never met before.

"This is my daughter," my mom said to the woman.

"It's so nice to finally meet you, Olga," the woman said to me.

"I'm Denise, her other daughter."

"You don't work for the basketball team?" she asked. My sister was a temporary usher for the San Antonio Spurs since a back injury and a drug addiction made it impossible for her to continue working as a hair stylist.

"No. I'm the teacher."

"A teacher?" she said. "What grade?"

"College. I teach English."

"Valencia," the woman said to my mom. "You never told us you had a daughter who was a *professoressa*."

I felt a rush beneath my feet. It was what I'd always imagined an undertow might be—something grabbing you by the ankles and pulling you along so fast you wouldn't have time to breathe. I was drowning from the inside out again.

She'd never even mentioned me.

The story I don't tell about my mother's death is from right before my husband took her face and asked her to give us a sign from beyond. I sat by her bed and stroked her arm, hoping she would feel me and know she was not alone. But when I touched her, she scrunched her eyes as if biting down on something distasteful and pulled her arm away. It felt intentional, not reactive, almost like she'd recoiled from something awful.

I never told anyone this happened. I felt shamed by her reaction and stupid that I had ever believed I was anything more than the child who was necessary for her survival.

My mother trusted me to take care of documents, doctor appointments, and damages caused by other family members. Yet I wasn't the child she spoke of with pride to her friends. Instead, it seemed I was a needed medication, important to her life, but not worth noting.

So when the check from State Farm came—when my mother finally gave a sign from beyond, I wasn't completely surprised it wasn't for me. She just wanted to make sure I'd take care of my sister's kid.

I'd been betrayed by blood.

Again.

THINGS THAT GO BOOM

My body, it seems, is erupting. I don't mean this in the metaphorical sense—like it's erupting with rage or into paroxysms of laughter—I mean erupting, as in blowing itself up bit by bit from the inside out. It's been happening for years. There's not much I can do about it either except, like Yeats, watch for some rough beast to slouch on by and plant another mine somewhere deep beneath my flesh. Then, just wait for the boom.

———

The eruptions began in my late twenties with a diagnosis of Polycystic Ovary Syndrome. During an ultrasound that was supposed to tell me why I couldn't get pregnant, my gynecologist picked up a pencil to circle images on a computer screen. Inside each circle, sat a tan-colored blob outlined by a white, shadowy line.

"Here, on your ovaries, is what we call the string of pearls. We look for this pattern in cases like yours." The doctor did not look at me, but at the screen instead. "This will make it difficult to get pregnant, I'm afraid."

I sat up to examine the screen a little closer. "Can you point to a pearl?"

The doctor took the end of his pencil and struck the sharpened lead along each circled blob.

I flinched with each strike, considering each cyst-like pearl a bomb waiting to explode each one of my dreams.

I sat back, away from the screen. "What do the cysts do?"

"Well," the doctor said, finally turning his eyes from the screen. "Lots of things. Nothing good for you, I'm afraid. They mess with your hormones, giving you more testosterone than you need. This causes hair to grow in places you don't want it to grow, like your back and neck, and hair not to grow in places where you do want it, like on your head. You'll most likely experience weight gain, acne, or dry skin, and more significantly, the lack of a regular menstrual cycle."

"So bad news for my husband too," I said.

The doctor cleared his throat.

After several quiet moments passed, I asked him about the cure.

"It helps to lose weight," he said. "But with Polycystic Ovary Syndrome it's darn near impossible to lose weight."

Boom.

"We could try some fertility treatments. Unfortunately, those have side effects too."

Boom.

"You're still young," he said, standing up. "Let's try the weight loss idea and see where we are in six months."

I knew where we'd be in six months.

———

After several miscarriages and an ectopic pregnancy where I lost a tube after developing toxemia, I managed to lose some weight. I got pregnant while on a cycle of Depo-Provera and worried the entire pregnancy about birth defects from the drug.

In the afterglow of delivering a healthy baby boy, I almost forgot about the silent bombs waiting to explode inside my body.

Then my father got sick.

My father was not a good man. Let's get that out of the way right away. Not only did he terrorize his family, but he keyed cars that were parked too close to him, switched price tags in stores so he could pay less for items he'd then give as gifts, and literally kicked dogs when they were in his way. Still, when he got sick and they admitted him into the hospital, all of us kids ran to his side. He did not deserve such love. We did it for each other, I think. We did it out of curiosity about what could fell someone so seemingly infallible. We did it because what else do you do? He was our father.

When the doctor came into the room, we were all cutting up, trying to pull salvageable stories from our youth out of a bag fraught with holes.

"Okay. There are a lot of you in here," the doctor said, standing by the door beneath a spotlight meant to stay lit in case of an emergency. We nodded in unison like some version of a family choir I'd seen on TV. He introduced himself as the cardiologist and we relaxed a bit. There was nothing strong enough to tackle my father's heart.

"Is it okay if I speak in front of your family?" the doctor said. My father nodded yes. "Your tests indicate you have stage 4 renal cancer. Your cancer has progressed past the point of treatment. As soon as I leave here, I am sending hospice in to meet with you. The prognosis for conditions such as yours is generally four to six months."

The doctor dropped his head and stopped talking. I worried for a minute he was going to take a bow—performance over.

"Might as well take me to Vesuvius and drop me in," my father finally said. "Cheaper that way."

Some of us laughed.

The doctor made his way out of the spotlight and out of the room.

"He's never even been to Vesuvius," my mother whispered to me, as if that was the problem with what he'd said.

"He was kidding," I told her.

"*Forse,*" she said. Maybe.

Mt. Vesuvius erupted close to once a century from 79 AD through 1037 AD. Then she fell silent for six hundred years. Our family has always had a strange fascination with Vesuvius. I'd guess it's because our family history mimics the history of Pompeii. Our family could live together in relative calmness for weeks, even months, until something would happen to make my father erupt and shower upon us the pent-up anger packed inside of him for ages and ages. In the aftermath of his explosions, there were casualties and scars to deal with, but, like the people who live in the shadow of Vesuvius, my family always came back, eager to rebuild.

This time, there would be no rebuilding.

We took my father home to die. He didn't go easily. In the last two weeks of his life, when he was at his weakest, he could summon superhuman strength at least once a day to try and escape. He'd take my mother's car keys, or sneak out the utility room door, or walk into the back yard to squeeze through loose boards in the fence. It got so bad that if the doorbell rang, we'd have to watch him like we used to watch our dog who liked to bolt whenever fresh air hit her face. My brother and I ended up being the ones who chased my dad home just to drag him back to bed so he could die where he was supposed to.

"He's running away from death," my mother whispered.

We nodded solemnly, as if somehow that made sense.

At night, we took turns sleeping at my parents' house. The hospice folks placed my father's final bed in the living room where he rested like a body already in state. At night, watching my father's restless sleep, I waited for the *boato*—the enormous roar a volcano makes when it blows. I wanted a dramatic moment before my father turned cold. I needed to feel the heat of his apology for the shattered lives he'd left in the wake of previous eruptions.

His restless sleep told me he was still roiling inside, but when he left this earth it was soft, like ash that can still suffocate long after the event is over.

Had my father simply been a bad guy his death might have been the end of him. It was more complicated than that. As often as he terrorized us, he also loved us. He was the parent who liked to play board games, ride the rides at theme parks, and find out-of-the-way diners where we could eat onion rings and drink malts while he told silly jokes. My father loved us unconditionally even though he could have killed us in his hottest moments of rage. His anger was one of those random things, like the path a lava flow decides to take.

A few months after my father died, my mother noticed a pimple growing out of the corner of my nose.

"I need to biopsy it," my doctor said. This was one of his last procedures as he had Parkinson's disease and was retiring at the end of the month.

As soon as he took the scalpel and cut the bump off my nose, I felt like the cartoon roadrunner when he realizes the trap door has been pulled out from under his feet. Pain. Sudden and intense. The numbing shot to my nose either hadn't gone deep enough or missed the mark completely.

I held my breath until my nose was patched, then ran to the sink in the little operating room and vomited and vomited, then vomited some more. My husband and the doctor stood back like victims on the news who later say, "We never saw it coming."

On the ride home my husband said, "I'll bet he's glad to be retiring now. That room looked like the set from *The Exorcist*."

I sat in shame and turned on the radio to drown out the memories of the day. Somewhere, I felt the familiar rumblings of Vesuvius.

When the doctor called to say it was cancer, I wasn't surprised. The bump on the side of my nose had erupted like a small toe on top of my nostril.

The surgeon explained the Mohs operation to my husband and me. He planned to remove the cancer, run a biopsy of the remaining cells, scrape more skin if necessary, and repeat the process until he was satisfied there was nothing bad left in the margins.

It sounded great in theory.

After the first run, the doctor stood at the procedure room door to tell me they needed to take more skin from my nose.

"No," I said.

"No?" the doctor repeated. He had already turned to walk down the hall.

"No," I said again. "I think I'm done. I want to go home now."

The doctor came into the room and rolled his stool toward me. "You have a large hole in your nose. I can't send you home with an open wound. Let's just finish this off today, huh?"

"I can't," I said. "My father died."

The doctor sat up straighter on his stool. "Oh. I'm so sorry. Did you just find out?"

"It happened a few months ago."

The doctor looked to the nurse, who shrugged slightly. How had that even come out of my mouth? Maybe it was the smell of the hospital or the desire to run like my father had wanted to, but in that moment I had a clear understanding of the futility in having the bad cells cut from me when there were so many layers and layers of memory that needed to be removed first.

I cried until the doctor went to get my husband from the waiting room.

With my husband by my side, I let the doctor finish the procedure and sew me up. I always wondered if the next series of scrapings really got all the cancer or if they just wanted me sewn up and out of there.

In a few months, I would see my surgeon on the news, arrested for molesting patients while they slept.

"You were never out," my husband said, reassuring me. But my concern was about what they'd done with the cast they made of my nose. Had it been left behind when the office was closed forever?

In Pompeii, many people were caught by surprise when Vesuvius exploded in 79 AD. Their bodies, smothered in hot ash, are preserved today in plaster casts. You can read the expressions of pain and shock and horror on their faces as easily as you can read a tattoo.

Somewhere, in some disgraced surgeon's office, there is a cast of my nose on a shelf, maybe even waiting to tell its own kind of story.

––––––

My body's newest eruption begins in my heart. In an instant, my pulse will go from a resting heart rate of fifty-five beats per minute to over two hundred beats per minute. Once my heart begins to run its private race, it simply will not stop.

"Paroxysmal Supraventricular Tachycardia," the ER doctor told me. "It's commonly known as SVT."

I had been at Target looking at patio furniture the first time my heart went wild. My husband ran me to the ER where they quickly did an EKG.

"We are going to use what we call a chemical paddle," the doctor said. "It's a way to reboot your heart using the drug adenosine rather than an electrical current."

I pictured a person standing over me rubbing two paddles together and yelling "clear," but it's not like that at all. Instead, the small ER room quickly fills with medical folks because this is an unusual procedure and medical personnel are curious. They also need several nurses and a doctor to mix the drugs and then administer them. With so many people involved, it feels like an emergency.

While the medicine is quickly plunged into my IV, everyone else checks the monitor that shows my pulse. When the IV is first inserted, the monitor shows my heart rate at two hundred and twenty beats per minute.

"Okay," the doctor said, standing up and holding my shoulder. "You are going to feel like a door is opening beneath you and you are falling through it, but you won't fall."

And it feels exactly like that. If you've ever been on a ride like Tower of Terror at Disney World, it's like you are standing on firm ground one minute, then free-falling to earth the next. But there is some chest pain. And lots of muscle contractions. Actually, it sucks.

In the meantime, people all around you are counting down. One seventy-five. One forty. One ten. Ninety. Seventy-four. It's like being a human New Year's Eve countdown ball.

After my heart rate is stable and the lab work comes back, they release me into the world. It only takes a couple of hours to stop and reboot a heart. Once home, exhaustion sets in. The hours of a racing heart, the muscle spasms, and fear finally kick in.

There are some tools I can use to avoid a trip to the hospital. I can bear down like I am taking a big poop to see if that will reset my heart. I can plunge my face into a bowl of ice water to see if that will shock, then reset the rhythm of my heart. I can pretend to blow into a balloon, which seems sillier than the other two ideas, but I've done them all. Mostly they work. Four times they haven't.

The thing about SVT is that you can have miniepisodes quite often. I've had a couple dozen. I've read that it's a good idea to avoid caffeine, sugar, and white wine. I've also read that it's an "electrical problem" and you can't help how you were wired so nothing really works except for an ablation if it happens too frequently. I've read and read and read about SVT because it's scary.

When I was diagnosed with PCOS, I blamed myself. It was my fault my body was messed up because I was fat. Because of my messed-up body, there would be no children. And even after we were fortunate to have one child, that child would be all there would ever be. My fault.

Boom.

I took the blame for the skin cancer too. The sun. The tans. All my fault. Boom.

But the SVT is different. I didn't do anything to get here. I don't think.

I worry about my heart racing whenever I take a plane, go out of town with people I don't know well for conferences, or hike deep into a mountain trail.

What will I do if my heart erupts into the wrong rhythm?

When will it happen next?

What is it I have lodged so deeply inside my body that it is trying to run away from me?

Boom. Boom. Boom.

I guess I do take some blame for this too.

After the first chemical paddle, my cardiologist sent me for a nuclear treadmill stress test just to make sure all was well. My appointment was scheduled at an old hospital in downtown San Antonio on the forty-somethingth floor. I am not a believer in ghosts, but that hospital was filled with them.

Waiting for my name to be called, I thought about how they would insert an IV into my arm, then insert radioactive material into that IV while I walked on a treadmill. I felt the building swaying. Looking out the window forty-something floors below, I saw a car that reminded me of the family car we'd had when I was a child. It was a light turquoise color, impossible not to notice. Ours had been a 1965 Dodge Dart. My father, always worried my brother and I would lean on the car doors and fall out, purchased external locks for the back doors. After we got in the car and closed the door, he would slide the silver locks into place like I imagined jailers turned a key.

After moving from Italy to the United States, my father joined the military where he made sure he had a job with summers free to travel. During the summer months, we drove across the United States and when it was good, it was the best. My father loved to sing and if he was singing Dean Martin, we would sing along. When I heard him start to moan "Endless Sleep" with that Hank Williams Jr. sound, "*I heard a voice crying in deep. Come join me baby in my endless sleep,*" I could see black clouds beginning to form in the car.

I've heard that some volcanic eruptions are soft with oozing streams of lava dancing down the side of the volcano like a Las Vegas chorus line. My father's eruptions were quick, like bricks being thrown through a window.

"I'm sick of this family," he would yell, out of nowhere, while we were driving on a mountain road without guardrails in Colorado. "I'm going to drive us off this road. Swear to God. All of us. None of you assholes deserves to live." With the locks in place outside my door, I was as good as buried alive.

My mother would cry gently as if the ash had already suffocated and rendered her useless.

Over the years my father would threaten to drive us off many roads and bridges, burn down our house, and poison our family. And though he never did, we lived in the shadow of the possible eruption.

"Ms. Tolan," someone dressed in white said from the hallway. "Are you ready for your stress test?"

"Sure," I said. "Can I use the restroom first?"

"Of course."

When she went back inside, I bolted to the elevator and to my car.

I never went back for the test.

Even the memory of a car can remind me that shadows never die. I can't go back in time and escape past eruptions. I can't go ahead in time to predict new rumblings. But on the day of the stress test, I saw an opportunity to avoid a minor eruption, and I took it.

These days, well over a million people live in the shadow of Mt. Vesuvius. Ancient Pompeii is now a modern city spelled with one *i*. People probably call Vesuvius a mountain instead of a volcano to make themselves feel better or maybe even to forget.

Experts say Vesuvius will erupt again. Some say it is past due for a cataclysmic eruption. In the meantime, the people who live near the volcano go to work each day and shop for groceries and possibly even go bowling from time to time.

Will this generation take the hit? Will it be the next?

When you live in the shadow of a volcano, no one is safe. Nothing is predictable. Things eventually erupt. Things eventually go boom.

THE UNDERSIDE OF NORMAL

From five houses down the road, I could see our garage door was open. From two houses away, I could see the slats of the blinds in the window of the house across the street held open like the sleeping eyeballs of a cartoon character. I knew our neighbor had the fingers of her other hand poised over my cell phone number, ready for me to pull into the driveway.

"He left the garage door open again," she'd say. "Third time this week."

With my own finger hovering over the answer button on my phone, I shut the door to my car and stepped over the boxes, old sleeping bags, and ice chests piled in front of my husband's car. One of the coolers in the driveway was a leaky one, but we could never remember which one, so we kept buying new ones. I counted four.

"Hey," my husband Bill said, popping out from behind an old futon he was pushing toward the car. His face was dirty and he was wearing a shirt that looked like he'd found it deep in the garage. "Come see what I did."

He took my hand and I followed him. Bill was as excited today as when he'd put together a swing set for our son when he was five. The night before, we had fought about how his messiness constituted a lack of respect for me. Today he was paying for his sins and I took his hand, willing to give absolution.

"All this stuff," he said, sweeping his hand over the coolers and sleeping bags and boxes in the driveway, "is getting sold in a garage sale this weekend. Everything else is completely organized inside the garage."

I followed him out of the hot Texas sun and into the relative coolness of the garage as he pointed out stacked and labeled boxes of our son's old Transformers and cartons of photographs I hadn't been able to look at since my mother's death a few years before.

"Nice work," I told him, squeezing his hand. "Thank you for taking this on."

"I'm going to do better—keeping things up."

I nodded.

"I mean it. You'll see."

"Okay," I said. "I really appreciate this. We can put the bikes back in here now."

He smiled. I recognized the smile he wore after twenty-plus years of marriage. It was the smile of pride in making me happy. It was still genuine and untarnished over the many years of negotiating my world.

I sighed and walked toward the house. "Long day," I told him. He grabbed my lunch bag and followed me. "I graded over thirty American Lit I papers today and twenty of them were pretty bad. Bad papers always take longer to grade than good ones."

He held the door open for me. I was grateful for the greeting the noisy air conditioner offered me.

"Hey," I asked, as he headed toward the kitchen to push the button that would close the garage door. "Did you happen to see my dad in the garage?"

"Your dad?" His smile changed into a look of concern. "Why would your dad be in the garage?"

"He should be in two white boxes somewhere in there. I think they're white. They would say 'human cremains' on the top."

As a kid, I'd been stunned into silence by the scene in *Fantasia* where Mickey Mouse puts on the sorcerer's hat and sets into motion a vortex of chaos. The idea of setting a broom in motion with the intent to metaphorically sweep the world away appealed to me. But as an adult, I understood the danger of intentions. I should have kept my mouth shut about the boxes filled with my father. If they'd gotten lost, no one would have blamed me. Instead, like the sorcerer's apprentice, I'd picked up the baton and set loose the past. I didn't want those boxes. Did I?

Bill looked out the window toward the curb where a long row of trash bags and boxes waited for a pick up from the city in the morning.

He shrugged. "I didn't know to look for him."

My phone began to ring. "Close the garage door," I said, seeing my neighbor's name on the phone.

———

When my father died in 2006, we'd already planned—my mother, brother, sister, and me—to have my father cremated.

"Would you like to share the cremains?" The funeral director asked as we all sat together in a small room. "After the cremation families often wish to retain a portion of the ashes for themselves."

This was an unplanned question and we sat in silence.

"I can split the ashes into thirds or even fourths," the funeral director said, as if the current concern was that someone might be left out of getting their share of ashes. "We'll have a ceremonial box available for the service."

"No thank you," my mother and I said at the same time.

From the corner of my eye I saw my sister and brother nodding yes.

"Okay," I told the director. "Split the ashes into thirds. One for him, one for her, and one for the cemetery."

The funeral director nodded. I felt shame at being a rejecter of the ashes.

Later that night, the three of us kids sat together on my back deck.

"He loved Savannah," my sister said. "I'm taking his ashes and sprinkling them there."

"I'm taking them to the coast where we went fishing," my brother said.

The wind blew and a few leaves fell from the tree above us. I knew no matter what they planned, I would somehow end up with at least one of their boxes.

———

My brother and I went to pick up the ashes. The lady at the funeral home brought us two of the boxes nestled in what looked to be a reusable grocery shopping bag with the name of the funeral home in blue letters across the front. The third part of the ashes were in a maroon, velvety-looking box.

76

"This is the ceremonial box," the lady who handed us the bag said. "We will deliver it to the cemetery for you, but I thought you might want to see it."

"It looks good," I said. "I mean, nice."

She nodded and placed the box on a table. I handed my brother the bag.

"Can we have another bag?" I said. "For my sister's box?"

"Of course," the lady said.

"Hey," my brother whispered. "Can you keep my box for a few weeks? I'm on my motorcycle and I'm not sure how it will hold up on a four-hour trip."

That box never left my garage.

Three years later, when my mother died, my sister moved out of my mom's house. She left her share of the ashes behind. I stacked her box on top of my brother's and left them in my garage.

————

After dinner, I pushed the button to open the garage door and grabbed a flashlight. My husband followed. Near the center of the garage, beneath the cartons filled with pictures, I spotted a white box. Behind it was an identical white box.

"There they are," I said. The box in front had black smudges on the outside. Ashes.

"I knew I wouldn't throw those away. Do you want to bring them inside?" my husband asked as I was walking back toward the house. He didn't really expect an answer.

————

The first holiday my husband spent with my family was normal. But I had forgotten how ill-defined that term was in our house.

Christmas Eve began with a fight between my father and my sister. In most families, fight means disagreement. In my house, it means fight. While Bill and I were busy watching TV or playing with the dog or talking to my mom, something happened to set my father off.

"Bitch," we heard my father yell. "Fucking bitch." It had to be my sister he was yelling at.

"Beppino," my mother began. "The food is almost ready. It's Christmas Eve. The lamp was from a garage sale." Then: "*Non arrabbiarti*." Don't get mad.

My sister and her youngest son, John, stood next to a lamp where the shade had a noticeable dent in it.

John was crying. "Papa, I'm sorry." He was missing his two front teeth from falling asleep every night with a bottle in his mouth. He was three years old.

My father grabbed my sister by her hair and spun her toward the front door. She scooped up John in her arms.

"Get the fuck out of this house. Animals," he yelled as he began pushing my sister in her back. "Goddamn animals."

My sister was trying hard to keep her balance. My mother ran to the back bedroom to get Olga's other two kids.

Bill stood with me in the kitchen. He was frozen for a minute, then, like someone had thrown a match at him, he began to move.

"No," I said. "You'll make it worse."

I reached for the car keys hanging from a hook by the kitchen door. It was almost a reflex, like crossing myself when entering a church.

When we were younger, there were many times my mother would have us run from our house to the car to escape my father's fury. If we made it out of the house, we'd sleep in the homes of friends. If we got caught behind the rage, it was like driving into a tornado.

I'd hide in my bedroom if we got stuck in the house. In the years when I still had a door, I'd hide even deeper behind a wooden room divider while listening to my father tear pictures off the wall, hurl plants and insults through the air, and pace the hall searching for someone to torture. I'd recite poetry, act out scenes from television shows, and create worlds where I was the leader. Sometimes I'd hike up my t-shirt and bare my belly like Jeannie in *I Dream of Jeannie*. There was power in having a bottle to disappear into. Samantha Stephens was another favorite character to become. With a twitch of her nose she could turn people into animals and bugs. If the noises in my house were very bad, I'd turn away from beauty and imagine having the power of Endora. Endora was not a woman to be messed with.

Of all the people in my family, I was rarely captured.

My husband was from calm, kind Norwegian stock. Bill was an outsider behind our foreign walls. What would I look like now that he'd seen our ancient rituals? Would he run?

In spite of the worry, I grabbed the keys. Survival instinct.

"Worse?" my husband said. "You said I'd make it worse? Worse than what?"

Outside the bay window we saw my sister fall onto the driveway and drop John. The little boy screamed, red-faced and snotty. My father kicked my sister in the small of her back as she struggled to stand up. My mother was trying to be calm, speaking in Italian, telling my father to stop—to come eat dinner—reminding him over and over it was Christmas Eve.

By the time it was almost over, my sister's three children were lined up in front of her car, crying in various pitches. It was like the saddest Christmas choir ever.

From the porch, my mother yelled to me through the open door where Bill and I now stood in the doorway. "Get a lunch bag for your brother."

I reached into the cabinet and told my husband to grab my mother's purse. We managed to gather everything we needed in time to see my father hit the roof of my sister's car over and over with his fist. He followed her car down the long driveway while the rest of us ran into the garage and got into my mother's car.

In the front seat, my mother put on her seat belt. In the backseat, I sat in the middle between my brother and my husband. My brother was hyperventilating. The lunch bag I grabbed helped calm his breathing.

My father stood in the driveway as we pulled out. He was yelling something, but we couldn't hear.

"Did you turn off the oven?" my mother asked me.

"I did."

"You did?" my husband shouted, as if he just realized we'd taken a wrong turn. His voice grew calmer. "In the middle of all this chaos you remembered to turn off the oven?"

"We've been here before," I said.

A few silent minutes passed while my brother breathed loudly into the bag.

"Where are we going?" Bill asked as we pulled out of the neighborhood.

"We'll drive around and look at Christmas lights," my mother said. "He will calm down soon." She began to sing, "*Rudolph the red-nosed reindeer.*"

My brother removed the bag from his face. He joined in the reindeer games.

"How long are we going to drive around like this?" my husband whispered. "Maybe we should get a hotel or something."

"No, no," my mother said. "Everything will be fine."

When we came back home, a note was thumbtacked to the front door. The note was not written in blood or in lipstick, but in simple red ink from a pen. It read, in big block letters, "Whoever sleeps in this house tonight will die. I will kill all of you, then set this house on fire."

There was a large space on the page, then the words "Except Bill."

My mother started to put the key in the lock.

"Mom," my husband said, looking at her as if she was about to walk into a fire. "Did you read the note?"

"Hey," my brother said yawning. "He said you were safe."

We laughed, my mother, brother, and me. We laughed because we had been here before.

We slept in the house that night and ate breakfast with my father in the morning.

"Are the kids coming back today?" my father asked my mother later that morning. "Tell them Santy Claus left them some presents."

My sister came over with the kids that afternoon. We ate dinner. We opened presents.

"This is not normal," my husband said at some point during the day.

"Sure it is," I said. "This is how it always goes around here."

He put on a good face and helped my mother with the dishes, but I saw him watching all day, waiting for the other shoe to drop. He was quick to pack the car the next morning and hug everyone good-bye. Back then, he couldn't imagine the kind of normal I had lived through.

———

My father wasn't ill for very long before he passed away. Before we knew that he was close to death, my husband's golfing buddy Peter had purchased plane tickets to come visit. The two of them planned to spend three days golfing.

My father's funeral was scheduled for the day Peter flew into town.

"He had one of those rates where if he changes anything he loses all the money," Bill said.

"It's okay," I said. "The funeral is early. You two can golf afterward."

There was the kind of silence that comes before a storm or before an accident or before a slap.

"I don't want to go to the funeral," Bill said. "You never let me say anything while he was alive, but I don't have to pretend anymore. I'm not going to honor him. He was a horrible man."

I took a breath. Bill had heard all the stories about my father by now. The beatings and the pain and the scars. He also understood that to see my mother, we had no choice but to see my father. But now that was over. No more pretending.

"You don't have to go," I said. "But I do."

"Bill might not be able to come to the funeral," I told my mother.

Usually my mother's expression was as familiar to me as a book I had read many times before. I could read disappointment or anger or sadness by the way her eyes widened, or squinched, or closed. But when she looked at me after I spoke, I found myself looking at a blank wall.

She didn't react.

"Did you hear me?"

"I heard you," she said, her eyes cool and steady. "He will be there."

"Mom," I said, standing in front of her. "I don't think he will. He hated Dad. He hated everything he did to us."

"I know," she said. "But he loves me. He will be there."

Bill showed up to the funeral with Peter, both men wearing golf shirts and shorts. Peter sat in the back row looking like someone who'd wandered into the wrong movie. He tried to look reverent, like a stranger in this strange land, but I was aware of how long it had been since an outsider had looked in on our family. How had Bill explained the sudden need to attend his father-in-law's funeral? What secrets did Peter now know?

In middle school I made the mistake of inviting a friend for a sleepover. That night, my father woke in a rage. When my mother tried to calm him by reminding him we had a guest, he was not deterred in his anger. He threw objects around the house, yelled at all of us, including the dog, and threatened to burn down the house, yet again. The girl who spent the night called her parents to come pick her up and never spoke to me again.

Normal people, like my friend, like Peter, are best left on the right side of normal.

After the final benediction, Bill hugged my mother and left with Peter, golf clubs rattling in the trunk of the car.

No one at the funeral asked who Peter was or wondered why he was there, because by now, with our family, anything seemed normal.

———

After the funeral, I suffered a series of illnesses. Sitting on the back porch one night, Bill and I watched the lights of the city come on and discussed the months since my father had passed.

"I think I'm getting sick because I'm detoxing from all the years of shit I had to eat," I said to my husband.

He didn't smile. "That might be truer than you think. How did you do it? With your dad? All those years."

"I loved my mom," I said. "It was a choice. She would have been punished if we'd stopped coming around because of him."

"Are you sure that's what it was?" he said. His voice was even, a perfect match for the warm evening. "Or was it easier to pretend you were just any other normal family?"

When too much time passed before I answered, Bill walked into the house, leaving me with a pile of truth at my feet. Had I taken the easy way out by finding joy in the pretense? What would it have cost me to walk away? To not play the same game everyone else had? Why had I needed this family?

I heard the sliding glass door open from the house next door. Soon, the couple who lived there began to argue. I couldn't make out all the words, but they sounded harsh and hurried and concerned his older daughter, who did not live with them.

I picked up my glass and started to walk back inside.

From outside our sliding glass door, I watched as Bill played his guitar on the couch. It had taken a lot for him to say anything about my family and to question why I had stayed so invested in something so toxic. Toxic for him as well.

I used to think I was brave to stay. I believed I was the protector, somehow, of the family. But I knew the truth. Bravery looks nothing like what I saw in the mirror. I stayed by my mother's side and added bricks to the veneer of our pretend house. I helped gather the materials our father used as weapons while all the time perfecting my role as Little Miss Perfect. By staying silent, I pretended to forget, forgot to forgive, and surrendered.

Sometimes, when I take out the Christmas decorations or store old clothes in the garage, I think about my father buried somewhere in the dark beneath unwanted junk and old clothing.

I haven't come very far, but unlike my husband, I always remember to close the garage door.

VISITING RENA

Each Thursday, the women made their pilgrimage to Rena. They carried offerings like salami or a new cheese, pictures of children or grandchildren, a letter from abroad or a recording of an old Italian song.

Whoever got to Rena's first would open the cabinet where the playing cards were stored, then stack the rubber-banded decks on tray tables around the room. After everyone arrived, the women spent hours playing *briscola*, taking breaks to dance together when a song they loved was played.

My mother came home on Thursday evenings looking like she'd been with a lover. Her cheeks were red from the food and the dancing and the wine, but her eyes were sad, like Cinderella when the carriage finally disappears.

During the school year, I never thought about my mother and her Thursdays. But in the summer, before I could drive, I strategically used Thursdays as a way to get from my house to somewhere else. Having grown up in Italy during World War II, my mother was not one to waste anything. Gas, especially, was not to be squandered on frivolous trips. If I wanted my mother to drop me off at a friend's house during the summer, I had to pay the price by going wherever she went first—the grocery store or the thrift shop or garage sales. On Thursdays, it meant spending the afternoon at Rena's.

"Did you call Lisa?" my mother asked. "Tell her I'll drop you off after Rena's."

I nodded and watched as she gathered things to put in her purse—coffee-flavored candies, a Kleenex, some pictures.

"Who are the pictures of?" I asked.

"Christine." My six-year-old niece. "She is taking swimming lessons. Rena might laugh when she sees the little bathing suit."

"She won't know you have pictures, Mom."

She closed her purse and picked up her keys. "How do you know what she knows?" She looked me over, then put her hand on the door. I smiled, knowing I must have looked good. If not, my mother would have ordered me to change my clothes or fix my hair. When the women at Rena's played cards, they threw down stories about their daughters to trump each other. Since I would be there in the flesh, my mom wouldn't be able to bluff. Looking good was one of the bargaining chips I had to use for the ride.

Rena's house was a ten-minute drive from where we lived. Turning the corner onto her street, I recognized most of the cars already parked in front of the house.

"How was she last week?" I asked my mother as she parked next to a navy blue Le Baron.

"The same," she said, nonchalantly, as if I'd asked how our neighbor was doing. "Pina thought she saw her move her shoulder, but that one always thinks she sees something."

Pina. The name made me wish my brother had come with us. We always sang the names of my mother's friends like an incantation: Lena, Rena, Pina, Tina, Nina, Gina, Dina, Nerina. It made the group seem less powerful somehow—their vigil less of a force.

"How long do you think they're going to keep her at home?" I asked, locking the car door before I shut it. My mom had been about to shut her own car door, but looked at me over the top of the car instead.

"What do you mean *keep her at home*? Where else would she go?"

I rolled my eyes as if I knew something about the world she might not. It seemed odd to me that the family left Rena, who was in a coma, on a bed in their living room like she was some kind of queen lying in state.

"Stand up straight," my mother said right before Rena's husband Rodrigo answered the door.

"I saw you coming from inside," he said, hugging my mother. Rod was a big, brown man with a short, military-like haircut. He looked like most of the men my mother's friends had married.

Rod stepped aside and the noise from inside the house grabbed me like someone pulling my hair. As I walked by, Rod awkwardly shook my hand and said, "Aren't you growing up?" I had just seen him a few weeks ago, but I nodded anyway.

Rena and Rod had three children. Two of them were grown and gone, but one son, Bruno, still lived at home. He was my age. He was also fat. Terribly, terribly fat. It was like he'd opened the worst of the teenage packages—acne, stretch marks, and greasy hair.

"Bruno's upstairs," Rod said. I hated to go up those stairs, but it was either sit with the women around Rena, or go find Bruno. Still, I hesitated.

There were no couches in the living room. Instead there was a king-sized bed with a mauve and seafoam green floral headboard in the center of the room. The women sat in a semicircle around Rena like an unorganized Greek chorus. Chairs of various kinds flanked the bed. My mother took her position in a dining room chair next to her best friend Marie, the driver of the Le Baron we'd parked next to. I went from chair to chair kissing each woman hello and collecting compliments like candy at Halloween. This was the one part of the ritual I enjoyed.

My mother took the pictures of my niece out of her purse and walked to the head of the bed. She kissed Rena on both cheeks.

"*Guarda questa foto*," she said, holding the picture in front of Rena's face.

"*Fa vedere*," Pina said to Tina, watching my mother. "Her eyes moved. Did you see? *Hanno visto tutti?*"

While the women took turns speaking to Rena, shuffling cards, eating, and singing, Rod silently went back and forth from the living room to the kitchen delivering cups of coffee and plates of food and bits of information to the groups.

"The doctor said she is the same," Rod told the group of women seated to the right of Rena.

"She's insane, Rodrigo?" Someone from the group on Rena's left yelled back.

"No, no—the *same*," he said. "Everything is good. Her blood pressure, her heart—all good."

86

"Pray, Rodrigo," someone else offered. "You never know what God can do."

He nodded, held his hands together like a prizefighter, shook them toward the ceiling, and returned to his chores.

On the edges of the bed, wooden trays held food, drinks, and cards. In the center of the bed, looking like a tiny sleeping mannequin, Rena served as an awkward centerpiece to this feast.

"Go say hello to Rena," my mother whispered, pushing me toward the head of the bed. I leaned over and kissed her forehead. Rena was warm and smelled like freshly applied hairspray. She had been tiny when she was still awake, maybe reaching 4'11", but I remembered her as a tiny tornado. Now she looked like a small child with an old face dressed in a pink robe with ruffles at the neck.

"Oh, no no no," Marie said, spitting something out into her napkin. "Rodrigo. Rodrigo," she shouted.

I stepped back from Rena, certain Marie's loud voice would wake her at last.

"What is it, Marie?" Rod said, coming out from the kitchen.

"You must go to the commissary this week. The prosciutto is in from San Daniele. I don't know what you gave us, but it is not the good prosciutto. I cannot eat this. *Mi dispiace.*"

"No," Rod said. "I'm the one who's sorry. I'll go to the commissary later. Next week you will have the good prosciutto."

Marie patted Rod's hand.

Rod looked around the room for an empty plate he could fill or a question he could answer. I saw how he might have been handsome as a younger man. He had a crew cut, but it was solid hair not in danger of falling away. His lips were a bright red in color, like he chewed on them rather than his nails, but otherwise he looked normal, not like a man who could render someone half dead.

The circumstances of Rena's coma were a bit beyond my interest level back then, but I had heard the story. In spite of his current role as the perfect husband and host, Rodrigo had been a player. For several years, Rena and Rod had taken in young girls from Rodrigo's village in

Mexico to help them around the house. That was not unusual, according to my mother, but the last girl they took in became the one who ended up helping Rod a little too much.

"Poor Rena," I heard my mother say into the phone when a friend called to tell her about the stroke. "It was because of Rodrigo and the girl, you know. The shock almost killed her."

"Mom," I said, in that tone I would never lose, the tone that meant she understood nothing about America or people or the world. "People can't make you have a stroke. There must have been something going on in her body. Did she have high blood pressure?"

She looked me in the eye. "When Rena saw Rodrigo and that girl in bed, she fell right on the floor. That girl washed the family sheets. Imagine."

I looked her back in the eye, but I wasn't sure then why the sheets were important. Later, I did wonder if a shock like that could cause someone to have a stroke.

"Did you find Bruno?" my mother asked.

"I wasn't looking." I replied.

She looked at me like I had been hidden under a sheet and suddenly revealed to her.

"You were born three days after him in the same hospital," she said to me. "Rena is like my sister."

"Well, Bruno is nothing to me, Mom. Nothing."

She cupped her hand as if to say she'd like to slap me, but then turned back to the cards. I walked toward the stairs. Bruno was up there somewhere.

When I was thirteen, Rena's sister came from Italy to visit the United States. Tina threw a party to celebrate the sister's arrival. There was a pool at Tina's house and all the kids gathered there. While we were swimming, a cute boy, older than me by a few years, swam in circles around me. He must have been the son of Rena's sister. We made small talk in Italian, then he asked me if Bruno was my boyfriend.

"*Certo che no*," I said. No way. My face reflected the disgust I felt for the question.

Bruno, just emerging from underwater, looked my way and ducked back in. I was sure he'd heard me. The boy who asked the question looked at me as if I'd stabbed someone.

"*Solo per chiedere*," he said. "I was just asking."

I got out of the pool and sulked in the shade until we left. It bothered me that anyone would think I could possibly be interested in Bruno.

I knocked on the door at the top of the stairs.

"Go away," Bruno said.

"It's me," I said. I heard some rustling, then the door opened. Bruno stood in front of me wearing an Italian t-shirt and basketball shorts. The light from the hallway landed on the pimples on his arms.

"Hey," he said.

"Hey," I said. He motioned for me to walk into the upstairs hallway. I followed him to the TV room and went to sit in the beanbag chair I normally sat in. As I went to sit, Bruno pushed me and I fell to the floor instead.

"What the fuck?" I said.

He laughed and threw himself onto the couch.

I settled into the beanbag chair. We watched a baseball game in silence. I'd almost dozed off when I felt a kick on my shin. Bruno was standing in front of me laughing.

"What's wrong with you? Quit kicking me."

"You don't like this," he said, kicking me again, harder this time. "Do you like this?" he asked, slapping me on top of the head.

I tried to stand up but he pushed me back down. "Show me your tits," he said.

"Let me up, Bruno."

He had his foot on my lap holding me down. He began to use his toe to pull my top up. "Stop it," I said, scratching his leg with my fingernail.

"Come on," Bruno said. "You like this."

I managed to get up and walk toward the hallway. Bruno grabbed my arm.

"What's wrong with you?" I said.

"What's wrong with *you*?" he said. "Your dad hits your mom, right? I thought you might be into that too."

For a moment, all I could see was the inside of my eyes pulsing with red. I tried hard not to move my face—not to reveal anything.

"Well at least my dad didn't make my mom have a stroke."

Bruno backed away. "That's not true," he said. "My dad didn't do that."

"Really? Because I heard your mom caught your dad fucking the maid. I heard your mom collapsed right then."

"You heard wrong," Bruno said. "My dad made a mistake, but he loved my mom. He never hit her."

"No, he never hit her, he just pretty much killed her. Everyone says so."

Bruno looked pained, like he was about to cry.

"Just go away," he said. "You've never liked me anyway. Why do you even come up to see me?"

I had the advantage now and I was going in for the kill. The secrets in my family had been around longer than the ones in his. I intended to keep it that way. "Because what else am I going to do when I come here? Sit around the bed and wait for your mom to wake up?"

Bruno bit his bottom lip and scratched his chin. "I heard the women talking before you got here," he said. "They were saying how your mom was so nice, how she didn't deserve a man as mean as your father. I was just messing with you, trying to find out if it was true. But now I know it is. You must be just like him."

Whatever happened after that only served to prove Bruno's point. He sat down heavily in the beanbag chair while I kicked him and called him names. I acted out a brief scenario involving the maid and his father. I showed him my tits and told him his father would love them. Then I left.

I saw Bruno four years later at his mother's funeral. He was fatter with less acne, but otherwise unchanged. He gave a brief eulogy about his mother's work with disabled children, then walked away from the podium. Right before he sat back down next to his father, he faced us all.

"When she looked at me," Bruno said, "she never saw anything but love. Now I'll never know that feeling again."

I avoided him after the funeral, even after my mother prodded me twice to go give him a hug.

When I went to the parking lot to get the car, Bruno was there smoking a cigarette.

"Hey," I said. I was in college then, slim and pretty.

He nodded, then flicked the cigarette behind his back.

"I'm sorry about your mom."

He smirked. "You think you're so smart," he said, "but you're just so stupid. All I wanted that day was to see your tits. All that stuff about your dad was bullshit. And guess what? I saw your tits. So who won?"

I had no idea how to answer Bruno, so I got in the car without saying good-bye and drove to the front of the funeral home where I knew my mom would be waiting.

"I saw Bruno," I told her as we drove home.

"He loved his mother," my mother said.

"He sure did."

"Such a nice boy."

I decided to leave it there, because at that point, I had no idea what winning even looked like anymore.

Terza Parte: Echi del Mio Sangue

PART THREE: ECHOES OF MY BLOOD

SNAKE LIGHT

After they died, he first, she three years later, we had an estate sale.

The estate sale lady told my brother and me to take everything we wanted out of my parents' house so she could price and sell what was left behind. It seemed like there might be some hard decisions to make, but there weren't.

Neither of us wanted the grandfather clock my parents purchased to commemorate their fiftieth anniversary or any of the furniture that had accumulated over the years. We both passed on the Babe Ruth collector plates my father had hoped would double in value.

I wandered through the house alone and found the wooden snake hidden behind the water heater in the laundry room.

"Look what I found," I said, carrying the snake by his coiled neck into the living room.

My brother looked up, then away, as if I'd found hidden porn. "Get it out of here," he said.

I laughed a little.

"I thought Mom threw that away," he added. "She should have."

Where there had been some discussion about the plates and the clock and the furniture, there was no question that the snake would be sold. I took the snake into the dining room and set it under the table, then thought better of that and moved it on top of the table. No need to startle the nice estate sale lady.

———

My father sent the snake to us while he was stationed in Vietnam. "A surprise is coming your way," he'd said, raising his voice so we could hear him over the noisy cracks and pops coming from his phone line in the war zone. He was shouting so we could hear him, but it didn't seem like information that needed to be yelled.

When the package arrived, my mother set it on the dining room table and waited for my brother and me to come home from school. We watched as she took her sharpest scissors from the sewing machine cabinet and cut across the top of the box, releasing the tape that would soon reveal the surprise. In previous boxes from our father there had been dolls under Plexiglas and Hot Wheels never seen by our friends before. My brother and I gleefully tossed all of the foreign-looking newspaper out of the box and onto the floor before we saw the content, and gasped.

In the box, looking right straight at us, lay a coiled snake carved in wood. He had sharp little green glass eyes and carefully detailed scales and a slightly open mouth. There was a hiss. There would always be a hiss when I remembered the story.

My brother, who was only five, jumped back, bumping his head on the doorframe. He began to cry, and my mother quickly closed up the box, shoving the newspaper on top of the snake. She put the box on the highest shelf of the closet in the spare bedroom.

"You know your father," she said to my brother. "He loves stupid things like that."

———

When my father returned to our lives, he found the box. In the kitchen, my mother whispered to him about how the snake made my brother cry.

"I'm making it into a lamp," my father said. "Who's going to cry about a lamp?"

He took the snake from the box and twisted its three parts together. Once finished, the once generic snake became a cobra rising tall, listening for unheard music. Released from the box, it was even more imposing.

My father tried to assure my mother that when he added the necessary pieces to make the snake into a lamp, it wouldn't look so bad. In the meantime, he suggested that placing the snake by the front door might scare burglars.

My mother found a corner where the snake could hide behind a rubber plant. She claimed the snake would look like it was in its natural environment. She winked at us.

We never felt protected from burglars or the snake or our father.

Sometimes at night, walking from the kitchen to our rooms, the light from a passing car would sneak into the living room window and strike the snake's glass eyes causing us to shudder, imagining what could be.

———

At the estate sale, we sold the clock, and the plates, and the snake that was never made into a lamp.

In the end, the snake became just another object that had seemed important until he was gone.

MERCURY RISING

I see my dead father from time to time. He drives through our old neighborhood in a late model Mercury, a little blue car stuck in the Game of Life. Sometimes I raise my hand in greeting, but it's the same kind of hesitant hand raising I did in school when I wasn't quite sure of the answer.

Not that it matters. My father never looks in my direction.

I have thought, from time to time, to turn my car around and follow him. Then I hesitate, like those who are lost. What would I do if he stopped and got out of his car? Would I walk to him, face up to him, say to him, *Dad, you've been dead since 2006. Did you really come back just to drive the same car on the same street in the same sunglasses?*

He is likely to shrug in response.

Would I beg for a morsel like a sad dog in a TV commercial? Would I whimper, *Daddy, have you seen me driving past you?*

But this is not a dream and there is never a time I turn my car around.

I'm not sure what any of this means.

———

I also see my mother from time to time, but only in my dreams. She is a newer dead than my father. I never have to beckon her, but I do stay watchful. She sneaks into the corner of my sleep carefully, like a child playing at hide-and-seek. She wants no part of stepping over the line, falling back into our world.

We talk as if time is nothing more than infinite spins on a game board. Sometimes she offers me wisdom, dressed up as guilt: *It's easy to love those who are easy to love.* Mostly she wants news about family and friends. And the new princesses in England. *I still mourn for Diana,* she sighs, *even after death.*

My mother is as interested in me as anyone is with a conduit.

Mom, I want to ask, *what did it all mean? Our family? Could we have taken another path?*

But my mother is a dream and I am here to transmit, not generate. I don't ask questions she might sigh about. Or answer honestly.

I'm not sure what any of this means either.

Still, from time to time, I'm afraid.

> Afraid I know too well.
> Afraid to end up a passenger in that car.
> Afraid to end up in the corner with my mother.
> Afraid to end up at the start of this game.
> Afraid.

A VERY SHORT HISTORY OF
ABUSE IN FIVE PARTS

1. Lucky Star

I was the only one my father never hit.

I asked my mother why.

You were born under a lucky star, she said.

Is that all I get from the star? I wondered.

My sister couldn't help me with this puzzle because like a modern-day Jack and the Beanstalk, she traded all her memories for drugs.

When I turned to my brother, he put his hand over the past as if it was a box of popcorn he would not share.

Why bring up the bad stuff? he said. *Why not think of the vacations we took instead? We had some fun then.*

He speaks something like the truth.

———

One afternoon, I sat with my mother among a display of lawn furniture at a local garden shop. It was hot outside, and we were happy to find comfort beneath the shade of an umbrella marked down to $69.99.

She was eighty-one years old.

Do you hear the birds, Mom?

She cocked her head. *No, my hearing for that is gone.*

Her voice sounded sad. Then she perked up.

But I remember how they sounded: Do do dee dee dee.

I laughed. She laughed. People walking by sent smiles like cool cocktails to the table marked $179.99.

It's so beautiful here, my mother said, as if we were at a resort.

We are the only ones who remember, she said, looking to the horizon at an imaginary sea. *You and me. We remember it all.*

I took her hand. She squeezed mine hard.

I'm sorry, she said. *They are all yours now.*

She would not live another five months.

She was right. I do remember. I remember every scream every plea every sound that pounded flesh can make. And even though nothing landed my way, I hold it all.

Alone now.

Lucky me.

2. Filament Fail

By the time my mother turned sixty, she was deaf in one ear and mostly there in the other. Every few years we made the pilgrimage for new, miraculous hearing aids. As she grew older, the trips became more like rites of passage.

In the waiting room of the clinic, she tells me: *I don't know if this is anything, but he hit me once, hard on the back of my head, and my ears rang. Then poof—gone. I couldn't hear out of this ear.* She points to the left side of her head.

The doctor calls us in and we go silent.

In the car, I ask why she never told a doctor about being hit.

What could they do?

I nod.

A few days after the left ear, the right one rang, but a little less.

I put on my seat belt and wonder why her ears went out separately, like light bulbs in two different lamps.

I consider the hits to her head. Even if her deafness wasn't his fault, it easily could have been.

Somehow, it's the possibility that burns.

3. Fast Flashback

My brother and I slept on our stomachs so we wouldn't see it coming.
   Our dad.
   His gun.
   What did we know?
   That he loved us, but hated her enough to do it.
   That he was a magician who could wound without ever touching.
   My brother and me
   Never talk about the fear.

———

He is a police officer now with his own gun.
   I never turn my back.
   We are tornado sirens in separate towns.

———

I'm not sure how my brother sleeps these days.

4. Someone Else's Past

Everyone has something, my mother would say after my father tore the house apart yet again. *Some men drink, some men gamble, your father, well*—she would point to various items in the house, as if I could just fill in the blank. What did we call what he did?

   Together we picked up the broken objects on the floor: a cuckoo clock, a picture of her sister in a shattered frame, crystal candies spilled from a broken Murano bowl. As we picked up each piece, she would tell me where it came from as if we were archeologists examining someone else's ruins.

   I got this at a garage sale, she said, handing me the biggest piece of the broken Murano bowl. *I paid $15.00. That was a good deal. You would pay at least $65.00 for that in the store.* She nodded once, emphatically, and I nodded back in agreement, then threw the glass in the trash.

   We don't have antiques in our home that mean anything. Everything we buy is a good deal from a garage sale or a thrift shop. Everything we own is someone else's past.

Mom, I said, when I was younger and one of her good deals ended up in my room. *I hate this picture. This is my room. You can't decorate it without asking me. And look at this frame; there's a chip in it. It wasn't such a good deal after all, was it?*

Oh well, she'd said, putting it back on my dresser. *What do you expect? Nothing is perfect.*

5. Wish List

Had I been my mother, I would have told me these five things:

1. You won't beat your own child;
2. You will finally believe you weren't adopted, but you'll still wish you had been;
3. You will always wait for the other shoe to drop—sometimes it will
4. Sometimes it won't
5. You won't be able to control it either way.

ACKNOWLEDGMENTS

Grateful acknowledgment to the editors of the journals where these essays first appeared:

Bodega: "Things That Go Boom," Summer 2019

Flock: "Visiting Rena," 2021

Fugue: "The Underside of Normal," Spring 2020

Lunch Ticket: "Betrayed by Blood," Winter/Spring 2019

Great Weather for Media: "A Very Short History of Abuse"

Mojave River Review: "Divisible by Thirteen," Spring/Summer 2018

The Penn Review: "My Mother Tells Me," Winter 2021

Santa Ana River Review: "Malocchio (The Curse)," Spring 2019

"A Very Short History of Abuse" was anthologized in *Birds Fall Silent in the Mechanical Sea*, edited by Jane Ormerod, Thomas Fucaloro, and Mary McLaughlin Slechta (Great Weather for Media, 2019).

"Betrayed by Blood" was a finalist for the 2019 Diana Woods Memorial Award in Nonfiction and the 2019 Penelope Niven Prize in Nonfiction 2019 (Center for Women Writers, Salem College). "Divisible by Thirteen" was a finalist for the 2018 Penelope Niven Prize in Nonfiction.

It took many years to find the courage to write these stories. I want to thank my husband, Bill, and my son, Andrew, for understanding why I had to walk this difficult path and for encouraging me every time I fell along the way. I love you both.

I also want to thank my daughter-in-law, Claudia, for her love and her strength, and for sharing her incredible Laredo family with ours.

Big thanks to the folks at CavanKerry Press, especially my editor, Gabriel Cleveland, for his unlimited kindness, creativity, and patience, and to Joy Arbor for her editing genius, sharp eye, and gentle guidance.

I have been lucky enough to find people on my journey who loved and supported me in ways big and small. There is no way I will remember to thank everyone, but here is my attempt: Julie Felux, Caroline Kuyumcuoglu, Venetia (June) Pedraza, Ito Romo, Carole Kyle Asbury, Erin Sherman, Barbara Guerra, Janie Scott, Jenn Lawrence, Baron Wormser, and Alexander Devora. I also want to thank my writing group, JP, Sara, Amanda, Julie, and Terri.

I'm not sure I would be here without my dear friend Dawn Gardner Simon. Dawn, you lived so much of these stories with me. Thank you for your love through all the messed-up years.

Special thanks to Bill Gaythwaite, my writer friend who came into my life when I needed him most. I met Bill when I wrote him a note about his story "A Place in the World," which I still think is one of the most beautiful pieces I have ever read.

They say if you hike the Appalachian Trail, you will stumble upon trail angels who leave supplies for weary hikers. On the literary trail, I have stumbled upon a few angels of my own. I will always love my Red Earth MFA Oklahomies. Kat Meads was my first mentor. Her sometimes kind/ sometimes sharp words powered me forward, gave me the courage to believe, and taught me to look for lamps by the side of my bed. Jeanetta Calhoun Mish is raw, honest, and the most fiercely loyal person I have ever met. Once Jeanetta loves you, you are loved forever. And then there is Allison Amend. Allison asks questions about your characters in a way that makes you feel she had coffee with them behind your back. And Kerry Cohen, a woman who lives her truth out loud and asks the same from you. These women are great teachers and even greater writers. Read them!

Often, literary angels surprise you when you least expect it. Thank you, Sherry Flick, Francine Witte, Alan Michael Parker, Gemini Ink, and the Writer's League of Texas.

A special note for the great poet and professor Ken Hada. Ken is the director of the Scissortail Creative Writing Festival, held annually at East Central University in Ada, Oklahoma. This festival offers writers the opportunity to participate in something like communion. If you can, offer them love and support.

I want to thank my Northwest Vista College family as well. I have taught there for over twenty years and have a deep sense of love for my campus community. The best part of teaching is my students, who every year make me believe there is a great future ahead for us all.

And then there is my blood—those of us left behind in the wake of all this pain. My niece and nephews, Matthew, Christine, and John. My great-niece Mya. My brother Greg. I love you all. I hope we can find a way forward. And to my cousin Pia, who might have guessed at some of this, but will be sad to hear the rest, thank you for the love and laughter you bring to our family.

Most importantly, I want to acknowledge the many women in this world who run, hurt, hide, and sometimes stay. You will never be invisible to me. If you need support, please call the National Domestic Violence Hotline at 1-800-799-7233.

CAVANKERRY'S MISSION

A not-for-profit literary press serving art and community, CavanKerry is committed to expanding the reach of poetry and other fine literature to a general readership by publishing works that explore the emotional and psychological landscapes of everyday life, and to bringing that art to the underserved where they live, work, and receive services.

OTHER BOOKS
IN THE MEMOIR SERIES

This book was printed on paper from responsible sources.

Italian Blood has been set in FreightText Pro, a typeface renowned for its historical innovation and ongoing popularity. It was designed by Joshua Darden, the first known African American typeface designer.

RESOURCES

Please take care when using these resources. In cases of domestic abuse, using private browsing while visiting these websites is advised.

Child Abuse

Break the Cycle
https://www.breakthecycle.org
866-331-9474

National Child Abuse Hotline/Childhelp
https://www.childhelp.org
800-4-A-CHILD (800-422-4453)

Domestic Violence

Battered Women's Justice Project
https://bwjp.org
800-903-0111 x1

Futures Without Violence: The National Health Resource Center on Domestic Violence
https://www.futureswithoutviolence.org
415-678-5500

National Domestic Violence Hotline
https://www.thehotline.org
800-799-7233

National Resource Center on Domestic Violence
https://www.nrcdv.org/ and https://vawnet.org
800-537-2238

Mental Illness and PTSD

National Alliance for Mental Illness
https://www.nami.org/help
800-950-NAMI (6264)

National Center for PTSD
https://www.ptsd.va.gov
802-296-6300